New Orleans Streets

New Orleans Streets

A Walker's Guide to Neighborhood Architecture

R. STEPHANIE BRUNO

FOREWORD BY WALTER ISAACSON

PELICAN PUBLISHING COMPANY

GRETNA 2011

*The word "Pelican" and the depiction of a pelican are trademarks
of Pelican Publishing Company, Inc., and are registered in the
U.S. Patent and Trademark Office.*

Library of Congress Cataloging-in-Publication Data

Bruno, R. Stephanie.
  New Orleans streets : a walker's guide to neighborhood architecture /
R. Stephanie Bruno ; foreword by Walter Isaacson.
      p. cm.
  Includes bibliographical references and index.
  ISBN 978-1-58980-874-4 (pbk. : alk. paper) 1. Architecture—Louisiana—
New Orleans—Guidebooks. 2. New Orleans (La.)—Buildings, structures,
etc.—Guidebooks. 3. New Orleans (La.)—Guidebooks. I. Title.
  NA735.N4B78 2011
  720.9763'35—dc22
                                          2010024076

Printed in Singapore

Published by Pelican Publishing Company, Inc.
1000 Burmaster Street, Gretna, Louisiana 70053

For my mother, Caskie "Kay" Brosnan Bruno, who saw the wonder of New Orleans and taught me to see it, too.

Contents

Section III: Across the River

Section IV: Along the Ridges

Section V: Back of Town

Foreword

New Orleans is a city of neighborhoods, and the surest way to appreciate them is through their architecture, block by block by block. Stephanie Bruno, the most passionate and discerning aficionado of New Orleans neighborhood architecture, takes us by the hand and guides us through just such a journey in this delightful book.

New Orleans came back strong after Katrina largely because of the resilience of her neighborhoods. After disasters such as that storm, it's commonplace to extol the fierce determination of the afflicted as they rise like a phoenix. But indomitable energy is not what earned New Orleans the sobriquet the Big Easy, and it has never been a phoenix in any sense. Instead, it savors the past even as it looks to the future. That served the city well in combining revival with restoration. Block by block, the city renewed itself authentically, rather than succumbing to master plans and developer-driven re-creations.

The best writers to have lived in New Orleans were William Faulkner and Tennessee Williams. However, my other favorites were two who knew the neighborhoods better. Walker Percy wrote about the savory malaise emanating from middle-class enclaves such as Gentilly and Elysian Fields. And Lillian Hellman recalled wandering up Esplanade Avenue below the French Quarter.

Hellman titled her second book of memoirs *Pentimento*, which referred to the brush strokes and old images that struggle to emerge from a repainted canvas. You see that a lot in New Orleans: advertisements for defunct brands of beer and coffee poking through the fading paint of old brick buildings. Indeed, it has always been a city of masks and painted faces, with past mysteries and glories lurking faintly visible underneath.

Like a pentimento, New Orleans has been a canvas repeatedly repainted. But its denizens usually take care to preserve the previous layers and let them guide the new brushstrokes.

Stephanie Bruno has been an exemplar of this neighborhood preservation sensitivity. It's a delight to walk with her—through Broadmoor and Back of Town, Tremé and the Irish Channel, Arabi and

Algiers—as she spots a distinctive decorative bracket on a shotgun or a cast iron vent on a camelback. This sumptuous book allows us all to share her view from the sidewalk and her passion for the neighborhoods that make New Orleans.

Walter Isaacson

Acknowledgments

When Renee Peck was about to launch the *Times-Picayune's InsideOut* tabloid in May 2004, she called me one day with what she said might be a crazy idea. Would I like to write a weekly column about historic New Orleans houses for the new publication?

Little did she realize that her invitation fulfilled my lifelong dream of writing for our local paper, if only on a freelance basis. Renee's encouragement and confidence in me has since led to many, many articles over the past five years, and I am forever grateful to her, the newspaper, and my current editors, Karen Taylor-Gist, Stephanie Stokes, and Mark Lorando, for the opportunity.

I learned most of what I know about New Orleans architecture from architect, author, and historian Robby Cangelosi of Koch and Wilson. He has patiently and efficiently answered questions through the years when I was stumped about an architectural style or foggy about a fact. What Robby knows could fill the Library of Congress many times over, and he has always been generous with his time and willing to share his knowledge.

When I am stuck and need an idea, I rely on my friend Louis Aubert, ASID, who has put his unerring color skills to use to brighten nearly every block in the city. We can spend hours together analyzing how a facade might be improved or color could be applied to highlight details.

Finally, I am grateful to my sons—Bruno and Jules Vetter—who have endured many detours and side trips to investigate an interesting house or check on a renovation. I tried to convince them that one day they would thank me for exposing them to exotic aspects of their native city that few ever get to see. That day hasn't come yet, but I can dream!

Introduction

I have long been enthralled by New Orleans and the wonderful texture of its everyday life. Maybe it's because I was born and have lived in the same house—a rambling Italianate center-hall cottage—my entire life. Many times, I have said this house exerted a paranormal influence on me at birth and influenced countless important decisions.

New Orleans Streets is a collection of photo collages and excerpts from stories that I developed for the *Times-Picayune* from 2007 to the present day and which have been published weekly as "StreetWalker: Views from the Sidewalk." Each "story" focuses on a single block in a neighborhood and explores step by step the architecture of the houses and choices their owners have made. Taken all together, they provide a snapshot of life in the neighborhoods in their endless variety.

The inspiration for the *Times-Picayune* column came from many "boots on the ground" visits to old New Orleans neighborhoods that I made over time, especially during my dozen years as the Operation Comeback director at the Preservation Resource Center. After visiting hundreds of houses all over the city, I came to the realization that our city's historic homes and streetscapes can only be appreciated properly on foot, from the sidewalk, and that speeding by in an automobile just doesn't impart the same rich experience or understanding.

I recall one night in particular that I understood this truth as never before. It was early evening and I was walking in the Garden District from my car to a reception a few blocks away. I was overcome by the beauty of the wide brick sidewalks, the height of the ornate cast iron fences, the fragrances emanating from gardens, and, of course, the complex architectural tapestry surrounding me. I recognized then that these homes and settings were designed in an era before automobiles and therefore had been intended to be experienced by people on foot.

In these pages, you will learn a little bit about dozens of New Orleans neighborhoods and some in adjacent communities. You'll get an introduction to the variety of residential architecture that lines our neighborhood streets and infuses our neighborhoods with indelible character. The Thumbnail Guide to Neighborhood Architecture should make it possible for you to make sense of what I've written and what you see when you're on your daily travels about the city. I hope you'll feel moved to explore interesting blocks on foot and to take a good hard look at the incredibly interesting buildings all around us.

The stories are arranged geographically, with consideration of whether the blocks are in neighborhoods flanking the Mississippi River or on other high ground. Another area, Back of Town, is at the geographical heart of the greater New Orleans area. The photo-illustrations accompanying the stories included many, but not all, of the houses on the blocks profiled.

New Orleans' fabulous old houses and some neighborhoods are imperiled as they have never been before because of the devastating floods that washed over the city when floodwalls failed during Hurricane Katrina. In a matter of hours, tens of thousands of homes, many historic, were rendered uninhabitable. Slow-moving bureaucracies, sky-high construction costs, uncooperative insurance companies, and a diminished population are all factors that have combined to leave many historic homes empty five years after the storm.

Only a heartfelt appreciation of what our built environment expresses about our culture and way of life can ensure the long-term survival of our precious neighborhoods and historic homes. Perhaps this book can play a small role in sparking—or reinforcing—such an appreciation.

A Thumbnail Guide to Neighborhood Architecture

Whether you're a lifelong New Orleanian or a Jazz Fest visitor from Los Angeles, you can't help but notice that our city's richest cultural traditions unfurl against a rather extraordinary physical backdrop.

For in the background of every second line, adjacent to neighborhood restaurants and music clubs, and framing our Mardi Gras parades are collections of visually arresting houses you just won't find in such abundance or variety anywhere else. They can be large or modest, stately or expressive, frilly or refined, but together they compose the visual context for life in New Orleans' neighborhoods. So keep this guide with you as you travel the streets and see if you can spot examples of the house types and styles that impart indelible character to our city streets. Before long, you'll be able to spout descriptions of the streetscape just as easily as you can whistle the opening riff to "Tipitina's" or explain how to make a roux.

House Types

Stripped of ornamentation, what shape does a house have? Where does it sit in relation to the sidewalk? Does its roof slope toward the street and back of its lot, or does it slope toward the side property lines? Does it have one or five openings across the front, and what does that tell you about the floor plan? Answer these questions and the guide below can ensure you will have a pretty good idea of what to call the type of New Orleans house you're viewing.

Creole Cottages

The Creole cottage is one of the oldest house types you'll find in New Orleans. Found most often in neighborhoods like the Vieux Carré, Tremé, and Faubourg Marigny, the Creole cottage has a roofline that slopes to the front and to the back, with gables on the side. Most are built at the front property line, right up to the sidewalk, and have four openings across the front.

Shotgun Houses

Certainly the most plentiful house type in New Orleans, the shotgun fits perfectly in the long, skinny lots that early developers laid out when they subdivided their family plantations. Shotguns have rooflines that slope to both sides rather than to the front and the back and, in their most elemental form, are just one room wide without an inside hallway.

There are abundant variations on the one-room-wide theme. One is the sidehall shotgun: three openings across the front, including a door that opens to a hallway down one side.

Another is the double shotgun, a duplex having two one-room-wide living units sharing a wall down the middle and having four openings across the front. And if you run across a shotgun house that's one story tall in front but two stories tall in back, you've found a camelback.

Townhouses

Townhouses are two-story buildings, often masonry, and found most commonly in neighborhoods like the American Sector of the Central Business District, the French Quarter, and Faubourg Marigny. Some had commercial space on the ground floor and living quarters above. Townhouses are built at the front property line and have a cantilevered balcony on the second floor. There are three openings across the front including a door that opens to a sidehall and stairway to the second floor.

Double-Gallery Houses

The double-gallery house is a direct descendant of the townhouse, adapted for neighborhoods where lots are larger and the character is more residential than urban. Like the townhouse, it is two stories tall with three openings across the front and has a side hall and interior stair to the second floor. But because it is situated on a deeper lot and is set back from the sidewalk, there is room for covered porches (or galleries) across the front at both the first and second floors as well as a front garden.

The Garden District, Lower Garden District, and Esplanade Ridge are great places to spot these houses.

Center-hall Houses

Center-hall houses can be identified by the five openings across the front, comprising a door in the middle (leading to a central hallway) flanked by two windows on either side.

Most have rooflines similar to those of Creole cottages—sloping to the front and back with gables on the sides. This house type is usually found in the Garden District, Uptown, Carrollton, and Esplanade Ridge set back from the sidewalk with a full-width front porch. However, there are a handful of masonry center-halls in the French Quarter, Faubourg Marigny, and Tremé without a setback or front porch.

Raised-Basement Houses

Our high water table makes it nearly impossible to have a subsurface basement in New Orleans, so our forebears invented the raised-basement house in the early twentieth century. A uniquely New Orleans house type, it consists of a lower-ceilinged "basement" built at ground level with higher-ceilinged living space above. Carrollton, Mid-City, and Broadmoor are home to hundreds of examples of raised-basement houses, identifiable by the prominent stairs that lead to the living space on the second level.

Bungalows

Though the bungalow isn't a distinctly New Orleans house type, many fine examples of this twentieth-century house type add considerable visual interest to neighborhoods like Gentilly Terrace, Broadmoor, and Edgewood Park. Bungalows have asymmetrical facades and floor plans and are often built in the Craftsman style. Though some students of New Orleans architecture use the term "bungalow" to refer to the house style as well as the house type, it's used here to describe the floor plan only.

The Elements of Styles

Ornamentation applied to the exterior of a house helps categorize it by style and offers clues to the era in which it was built. For just as clothes styles go in and out of favor over time, so too do architectural styles.

In the street walks that follow, the styles you'll encounter most often include Creole (before 1830), Greek Revival (1830-1860), Italianate (1860-1880), Eastlake and Queen Anne (1880-1910), and Craftsman (1910-1940). Other Revival styles—Colonial, Neoclassical, and Mediterranean—overlapped with the Craftsman style.

What to Look For

Greek Revival
- Box columns
- Clean, horizontal lines
- Greek Key-patterned door surrounds
- Entablature with dentil work

Italianate
- Paired brackets over square or round columns
- Arched-top windows, transoms, and door glass
- Corbels in the entablature

Eastlake
- Turned wood columns
- Frieze of piercework panels and spindles
- Spandrels
- Milled brackets

Craftsman
- Exposed rafter tails
- Deep eaves with post or angle brackets
- Windows and doors with asymmetrical patterns
- Flared box columns, often atop masonry pedestals

Revival Styles
- Colonial Revival
- Neoclassical Revival
- Mediterranean Revival

New Orleans Streets

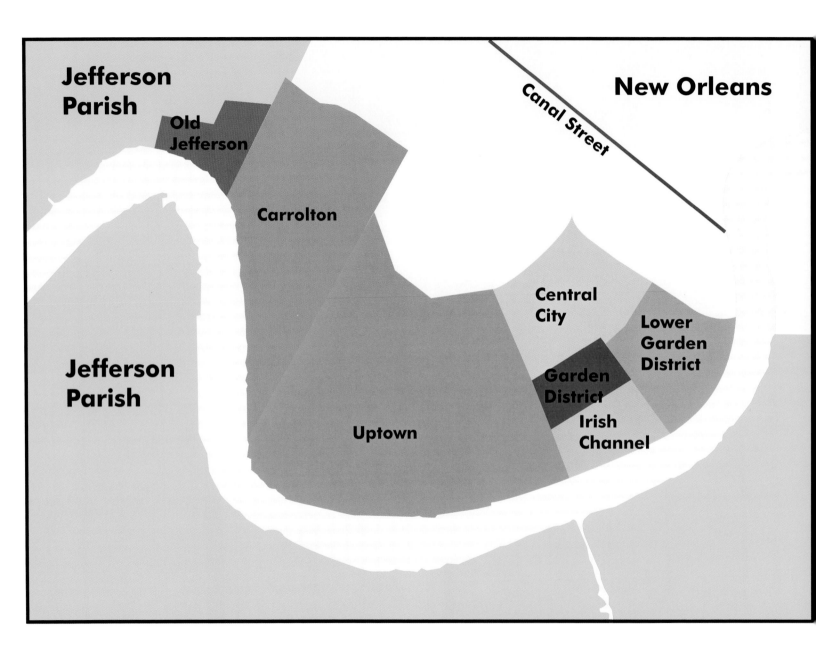

SECTION I
UPRIVER OF CANAL STREET

Uptown, downtown, river, lake—these are the four points of the compass in the New Orleans area. The earliest communities, be they in Jefferson, Orleans, St. Tammany, or St. Bernard parishes, were all established to take advantage of one body of water or another.

Much has been said and written since Hurricane Katrina about the wisdom of building on the "high ground," the sliver by the river, and so forth. But "high" is a relative term in a mature river delta like that of the Mississippi River. For even thousands of years of springtime floods could build the natural levee of the river to no more than ten to twenty feet or so, meaning the difference between low ground and high ground here can be measured in tens of feet rather than hundreds as it is in other parts of the country.

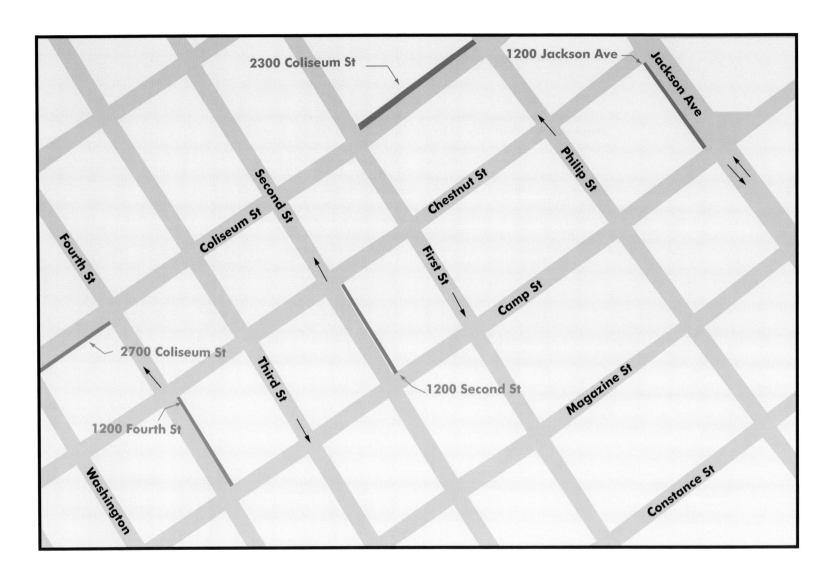

2300 Coliseum St

1200 Jackson Ave

Jackson Ave

Second St

Coliseum St

Chestnut St

Philip St

Fourth St

First St

Camp St

2700 Coliseum St

Third St

1200 Second St

1200 Fourth St

Magazine St

Washington

Constance St

Garden District

The Garden District was added to the National Register of Historic Places in 1974 and today is known internationally for its history and architecture. Though boundaries are often debated, the National Register perimeter is Carondelet Street on the north, Magazine Street on the south, Josephine Street on the east, and Louisiana Avenue on the west.

The neighborhood encompasses parts of several former plantations, including a portion of the Panis Plantation, which were eventually subdivided into faubourgs and then incorporated as the City of Lafayette in 1832. The City of Lafayette, in turn, was annexed to New Orleans in 1852.

The Panis Plantation was a pie-shaped plot of land bounded by present-day Josephine and Philip streets extending from the swamp on the north to the river on the south. When Madame Panis subdivided the southern portion of the plantation into Faubourg Panis in 1813, she named the broad thoroughfare that served as its axis Cours Panis. But that was before January 8, 1815, when Gen. Andrew Jackson's astonishing victory at the Battle of New Orleans made him the hero of the city. By 1832, not only had the northern half of the former Panis Plantation been subdivided and folded into the new City of Lafayette, but Cours Panis had been renamed Jackson Avenue in honor of the battle hero.

2300 block of Coliseum Street

THE BLOCK: The 2300 block of Coliseum Street, on the odd-numbered or lake side of the street, between Philip and First, not far from the Louise S. McGehee School. The block is called Hall's Row for the collection of seven houses built by John Hall in 1869, based on plans by the esteemed New Orleans architect Henry Howard.

THE HOUSES: A row of seven sidehall shotgun houses. Likely identical when they were built, each evolved a little differently so that now no two are exactly alike.

Hall's Row is a bit of an anomaly. Unlike the many large homes in the neighborhood commissioned by their future residents, these houses were built "on spec" by John Hall, who intended to sell them off (though a colorful myth says he had seven daughters and built the houses as wedding gifts for them). Their lots are smaller than is common in the neighborhood, and the houses are of a more modest scale. Rarer still,

they were designed by one of the mid-nineteenth century's most lauded architects, the Irish-born Henry Howard.

ANATOMY OF THE BLOCK: No doubt, all seven houses on the block had a typical sidehall shotgun floor plan when they were built, though each has changed over time. Some have camelback additions, while others' side galleries have been enclosed or shortened. One or two have side entrances or additions.

The house closest to First Street has changed the most. Compared to the other houses, its box columns are spaced differently and the paired brackets on the entablature don't align with the columns themselves. Still it has something

the others don't—an especially handsome cast iron porch railing.

The next house has a camelback, maybe a later addition. The height of the entablature is enhanced by a tall parapet with a still-taller middle section, likely a feature that was present on all of the houses when they were built.

Immense spandrels between the columns on the third house create exuberant arches and infuse the facade with an Italianate flavor. About half the houses on the block have this feature. The fourth house has the arches, the parapet, and even a pair of substantial cast iron gateposts flanking the entry to the front yard. This house has a red door in a style that suggests it is original to the house.

The fifth house has a camelback but no parapet or arched brackets between the columns. Its neighbor to the right has both, plus something unique on the block: an unusual transom over the front door, with a pattern that looks like the spokes of a wheel. At one time, did all the houses have this transom? At the last house, I am taken by the garden and how it suits the architecture.

2700 block of Coliseum Street

THE BLOCK: The 2700 block of Coliseum Street, on the even-numbered or river side of the street, between Fourth Street on the east and Washington Avenue on the west. The block is in the midst of one of the historic district's most traveled areas, thanks in large part to the proximity of Commander's Palace restaurant and the fabled Lafayette Cemetery No. 1.

These days, anonymity would be pretty much impossible for the block, given that New Orleans patron and actress Sandra Bullock just bought a home nearby and much of Brad Pitt's movie *The Curious Case of Benjamin Button* was filmed here.

THE HOUSES: Five double-gallery townhouses designed by William Alfred Freret, son of a New Orleans mayor and cousin of James Freret, another star architect of the late nineteenth century. "Will" Freret, as he was known, designed many fine buildings in New Orleans and put his stamp on public buildings elsewhere in the United States in his role as supervising architect of the United States Department of the Treasury.

A plaque affixed to an iron fence on the block reads: "Freret's Folly. This row of once identical Greek Revival townhouses was erected in 1861 by New Orleans architect William A Freret . . . as a speculative building project. The row was so named after the Civil War made the venture financially unsuccessful."

ANATOMY OF THE BLOCK: Standing on the corner of Coliseum and Fourth, I like to think about Freret standing in the same place, eyeing his row of five townhouses, then pivoting to admire his grand creation, the Eustis mansion, catty-corner to the row. Even if he was not a vain man, he must have felt somewhat vindicated that his former "folly" had survived and was in the best of company.

Although all five of the double-gallery townhouses were built to look alike, each has changed a bit over the past 150 years. All are two-story raised houses with three openings across the front, top and bottom. A porch or gallery extends the width of the house at both levels. The entry is to the left—a recessed door with a segmental arch and pilasters to emphasize its importance.

Windows are floor to ceiling and no doubt open high enough to allow residents to walk out onto the gallery. There are box columns with applied square molding on the first floor and Corinthian columns in the "Tower of Winds" pattern above. Shutters with operable louvers screen the windows, and a handsome cast iron balcony rail completes the composition.

On one house, I notice paired corbels over each of the columns. Everything I have read about these houses says they are Greek Revival, but aren't those paired corbels an Italianate feature?

1200 block of Fourth Street

THE BLOCK: The 1200 block of Fourth Street, on the odd-numbered or east side of the street, between Chestnut Street and Camp Street, not far from Magazine Street to the south and the oft-visited Lafayette Cemetery No. 1 on Washington Avenue nearby.

THE HOUSES: Five houses of varying architectural types and styles, including a Greek Revival double-gallery house, an Italianate raised center-hall, a well-proportioned twentieth-century house, and three two-story houses (one single and two doubles) in a flamboyant style that blends Eastlake and Queen Anne detailing. All are set back from the sidewalk behind wrought iron fences.

ANATOMY OF THE BLOCK: I start at the corner of Chestnut and walk toward Magazine, stopping first to admire the Greek Revival townhouse at the corner. It has a side gallery—an unusual feature on a house of this type—and a semioctagonal bay facing an immense side yard. I spot the dentils in the entablature and look for more Greek Revival features before I notice the "Greek Key" door surround marking the entry on the right.

True to classic double-gallery form, there are three full-length openings across the front. Adding to the appeal is the herringbone-patterned brick sidewalk that stretches from the iron fence to the curb—no planting strip interrupts it.

Next door is a raised center-hall on an oversized lot. I describe it as Italianate because of the paired brackets over the columns and the modillions on the entablature, but unlike many Italianates, it does not have arched top windows and doors. So I revise my description to say it is transitional between one style and another. Dormers, the center one much larger and closer to the front of the house than the two flanking it, add a vertical element to what would otherwise be a low, horizontal profile.

I continue along the herringbone sidewalk and reach a third house, set back from the sidewalk behind an iron fence like its neighbors. Elegantly proportioned and featuring a nicely detailed recessed entry, this house likely was built in the early twentieth century, perhaps on a side lot that once belonged to one of the houses on either side of it. If not, if it is an earlier house, it has changed so much over time that I, at least, have a hard time figuring out what it once may have looked like.

The mood shifts when I reach the next three houses. In lieu of restrained ornamentation, these three are decked out in all manner of millwork, from complex railings composed of sawn and turned wood elements to oversized semicircular windows to unusual column brackets that impart a Moorish flavor to the composition. Add scalloped shingles, multipaned windows with stained glass, and fluidly shaped rafter tails and the result is a highly original and visually captivating composition.

1200 block of Jackson Avenue

THE BLOCK: The 1200 block of Jackson Avenue, on the even-numbered or west side of the street, between Chestnut Street on the north and Camp Street on the south, close to Trinity Episcopal Church and school. According to geographer Richard Campanella in his 1999 book *Time and Place in New Orleans,* "Tree lined Jackson Avenue was a prestigious address in the nineteenth century and today boasts some of the most splendid mansions in the area. Now the lower limit of the Garden District, it forms an impressive path to the river and a prominent spoke in the radiating street pattern of uptown New Orleans."

THE HOUSES: Four "splendid mansions" on large lots, built in styles of the mid to late nineteenth century. Although the Italianate style dominates, a couple of the houses hint at the Queen Anne and Eastlake styles to come. Every house on the block is fronted by an iron fence with substantial posts, very likely original to the houses.

ANATOMY OF THE BLOCK:

There is so much architectural territory to cover on this block that I soon realize that I will have to focus on a few defining elements on each house. So I start with the two-story center-hall on the corner of Camp and consider what elements define it. I spy Italianate features, like the curved-top windows and shutters on the left half of the house and arched-top front doors, and intriguing millwork wherever I look.

The styling is transitional—not purely Italianate and not quite Eastlake or Queen Anne. The columns, for instance, are generally square but with chamfered edges and raised panels. Where the turned balustrade connects to the columns, a circular medallion appears on the face of each. Fancy corbels are present at the tops of the columns. The dormer has applied carving in the gable and complex pilasters.

The next house sits back on the adjacent lot, behind a pair of stately iron gates that perhaps served a carriage house in the past.

In its basic form, it's a two-story sidehall residence, a townhouse. But what makes it especially appealing is the massing. Rather than flat planes on all sides, there are features like terraces, porches, a recessed entry, and balconies, all of which produce a visual rhythm.

The dynamism of the massing is enhanced by the recessed wing on the right-hand side, visually unified with the main portion of the house by the deep eave and brackets below it. The original columns seem to be missing on the recessed wing's balcony, but on the main facade, the columns are a variation of Corinthian—Tower of Winds—and the brackets are paired over each.

The fourth house is a raised center-hall house, as much as seven feet off the ground. A few notable elements are the bay on the left side, the cast iron railing with its delicate lyre pattern, and the handsome recessed entry flanked by pilasters with egg-and-dart patterned molding on their capitals. The bay is especially

intriguing because the entablature wraps around it at the top.

I reach the corner of Jackson and Chestnut and the last splendid mansion on the block. This one is set much farther back from the sidewalk than its three neighbors, with an expanse of green in front and to the left. On the right, along Chestnut, the canopy of an elaborate porte-cochere extends toward the street.

Because of the hedge at the front property line, the only way to get a good long look at all of the home's features is to peer through the gate. When I do, I see highly detailed columns to rival those of the first house on the block, plus complex massing of volumes to match that of the second house. I see that the porch extends across the width of the front then wraps around both the right and left sides where prominent bays are located. It occurs to me that this house incorporates some of the finest elements of all the other houses on the block, recombined to produce a totally original composition.

1200 block of Second Street

THE BLOCK: The 1200 block of Second Street in the Garden District, on the odd-numbered or east side of the street, between Chestnut Street on the north and Camp Street on the south. Magazine Street and its wealth of commercial venues is just a block or so away.

THE HOUSES: Three freestanding houses and one that may be part of a larger complex. The two houses closest to the corner of Chestnut are twins, Greek Revival/Italianate double-gallery residences likely dating to the 1860s or so. A later stucco house sits behind a vine-covered wall.

ANATOMY OF THE BLOCK: I start at the corner of Chestnut and Second and walk south toward Magazine. The first two houses are especially large double-gallery houses; in addition to the main portion of the house, each has a recessed wing on the left side, probably one-room wide but as deep as the main portion of the house. Walk-through windows appear at both levels of the recessed wing, offering access to a narrow gallery when opened. In all likelihood, these are "slip-head" windows, the kind that slide up into a pocket in the wall above so that you can open the windows above head height and walk out through the opening.

I'm on the hunt for examples of Greek Revival and note the details on these two houses that fit that style. The trim around both front doors is in the Greek Key pattern—wider at the top, then narrowing before flaring out as it extends to the decking on the first-floor gallery.

The chaste box columns, free of ornamentation and rectangular in section, also adhere to the austere principles of the Greek Revival style. There are no fluted embellishments, no fancy capitals.

But as my eyes rise to the entablature above the second-floor columns, I see a mix of Greek Revival and Italianate elements. As I would expect in Greek Revival, I see a row of dentils beneath the cornice, but I also see pairs of curvaceous brackets that sit under the cornice above each column. I also spot a curved top on the raised center section of the parapet. Both the brackets and arched parapet are clues that the Italianate style was coming into vogue when this building was constructed and that it influenced decorative choices.

A few steps farther down the block are two more residences, both almost hidden behind garden walls. Part of the first house peeks above its vine-covered masonry wall high enough to reveal a gabled stucco facade with a large, multipaned window with a fan light on top. A rose vine in bloom climbs the iron trellis above the masonry pillars at the entry, and I see a winding path of flagstone leading to the front door. Beyond these details, the home's secrets are expertly concealed.

Closer to Camp Street, a white gate set in a masonry wall leads to another private garden. The house number on the wall tells me that there is a residence beyond, but from my vantage point, I can't tell if it refers to the two-story service wing straight ahead or the smaller two-story outbuilding to the left of the gate.

Lower Garden District

The Lower Garden District was added to the National Register of Historic Places in 1972 and was also designated a local historic district regulated by the Historic District Landmarks Commission. The area is bounded roughly by St. Charles Avenue on the north, Tchoupitoulas Street on the south, Calliope Street on the east, and Josephine Street on the west.

Recognized for its extensive collection of mid-nineteenth-century residences, the Lower Garden District is centered on Coliseum Square, a leafy retreat offering neighborhood residents and visitors a venue for picnics, dog walks, and other leisurely activities. The square and streets around it were laid out in 1809 by the deputy city surveyor and Frenchman Barthelemy Lafon, who envisioned fountains, markets, churches, schools, and more for this urban neighborhood. One source credits Lafon's love of Greek mythology as the reason neighborhood streets are named for the nine muses.

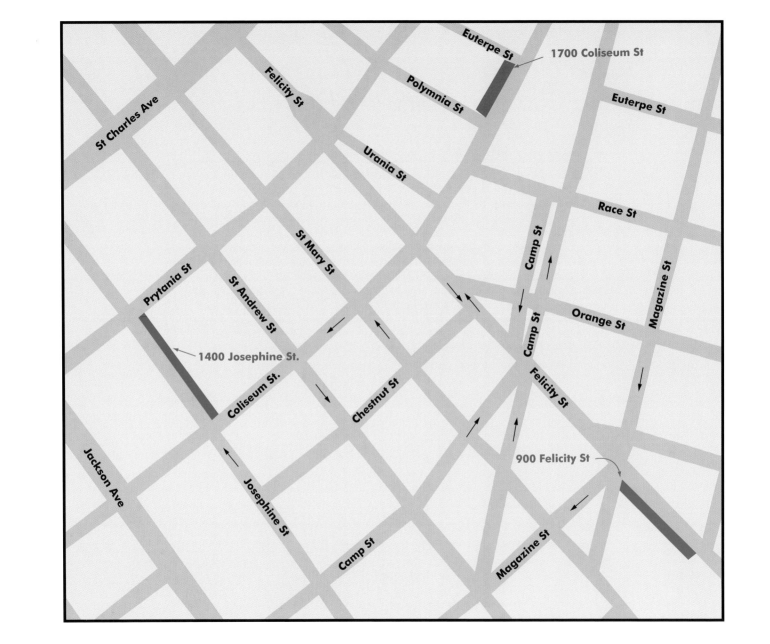

1700 block of Coliseum Street

THE BLOCK: The 1700 block of Coliseum Street, on the odd-numbered or north side of the street, between Euterpe on the east and Polymnia Street on the west. The block faces Coliseum Square and is situated just a couple of blocks from the St. Charles Avenue streetcar line in one direction and the galleries and restaurants of Magazine Street in the other.

THE HOUSES: Four very different homes line this block, ranging in date from the 1830s to 1950s and expressing styles and forms from their respective eras. The collection includes a 1½-story raised center-hall villa, a two-story Greek Revival townhouse with a semioctagonal bay, a one-story stucco house with an apparently twentieth-century pedigree, and a two-story townhouse that was likely updated in the Eastlake era.

ANATOMY OF THE BLOCK: At the corner of Coliseum and Polymnia stands the Goodrich-Stanley House, a local landmark named in part for Sir Henry Morton Stanley. He was the explorer and journalist who went to Africa to cover the search for the missing Scottish explorer David Livingstone and who, upon finding him, reportedly delivered the greeting: "Dr. Livingstone, I presume?" This 1830s-era center-hall house was moved to this location from Orange Street in about 1970 to prevent its demolition.

Next door is a double-gallery townhouse, in stucco. Though the embrace of a mammoth oak obscures some elements, its chaste details and restrained ironwork are enough for me to conclude it is built in the Greek Revival style.

A few steps closer to Euterpe, I find a one-story stucco house with a balustrade running along its flat roofline. Though it appears to be from the twentieth century, it blends surprisingly well with the older homes on the block because of thoughtful detailing like the recessed entrance and elongated windows.

The house on the corner of Coliseum and Euterpe breaks all the rules of the block. It sits right on the sidewalk, whereas its neighbors sit back behind fences. It has no side yard at all, though the others are situated on wide lots. And as for style, it combines elements of Greek Revival, Italianate, and Eastlake. My bet is that it is a mid-nineteenth-century townhouse fashionably updated several times to produce an exuberant and idiosyncratic composition.

1400 block of Josephine Street

THE BLOCK: The 1400 block of Josephine Street, on the odd-numbered or east side of the street, between Prytania Street on the north and Coliseum Street on the south. Just a block away in one direction is Trinity Church on Jackson Avenue. A few blocks in another direction is the Magazine Street commercial district. At one end of the block, facing Prytania, is a corner grocery.

THE HOUSES: A trio of houses on large lots, including a quasi-Italianate center-hall house, a Greek Revival double-gallery house, and a Gothic Revival townhouse. These generously proportioned houses sit far apart from one another and well back from the sidewalk.

ANATOMY OF THE BLOCK: When I arrive on the 1400 block of Josephine Street, it seems almost too good to be true. There's the classic Greek Revival double-gallery house smack in the middle of the block. Even better, it is flanked by extremely distinctive houses, a raised center-hall on the left with both Greek Revival and Italianate

elements and a townhouse on the right in the Gothic Revival style (very rare in residential architecture in New Orleans).

I start at the north end of the block with the center-hall house, raised about five feet off the ground and having a massive set of steps leading up to the front porch and entry. Like most center-halls, this one has a "cottage" roofline—a roof that slopes toward the front and the back and has side gables. The box columns and entablature are Greek Revival in nature, but this house also has paired brackets over the columns and such an elaborate dormer that it's clear the Italianate style has asserted itself. The dormer alone gives it away

with its arched and paired windows and scrolled brackets buttressing it.

Next door is the Greek Revival double-gallery house with spare, almost severe, detailing. Dentil work in the cornice and a handsome cast iron railing are present but no more embellishment than that.

I continue to the fanciful Gothic Revival house closer to Coliseum Street, a rare find in New Orleans. By the looks of it, Hurricane Katrina may have caused the building to lean a bit. I see supports and braces here and there and notice that some decorative elements, like the brackets that form the pointed arches between the lower columns, are missing. However, there is no mistaking the Gothic Revival characteristics of the house, such as its steeply pitched roof with a front gable, milled brackets on the roof overhang, carved wood elements at the gable peak, and spandrels between the first-floor columns that, together, form a pointed arch.

A variation of Gothic Revival called Carpenter Gothic may also be expressed. The term derives from the practice of using wood to imitate other materials, and I note that heavy moldings around the gable window mimic the carved stone reliefs one might see on a church. Wood cutouts applied to simple wood pickets on the porch railing imitate a cast iron balustrade, another Carpenter Gothic trick. The most unusual element of all, though, is the "gingerbread" between the tops of the thin columns on the second floor. I would expect them to be made of wood and cut with a scroll saw. Instead, the element is stamped and punched metal.

900 block of Felicity Street

THE BLOCK: The 900 block of Felicity Street, on the even-numbered or west side of the street, between Hastings Place on the north and Laurel Street on the south. Felicity Street retains its historic character here, thanks in part to the paving stones used to form the roadway.

The block is in a sector of the Lower Garden District between Magazine and Tchoupitoulas where residential, commercial, and institutional buildings mix with one another. River Gardens, a gleaming new community built on the site of the former St. Thomas Housing Project, is just around the corner. The historic and ornate St. Mary's Assumption Church, St. Alphonsus Cultural Center, and Kingsley House are landmarks close by.

THE HOUSES: Ten buildings including a church, three two-story houses, five double-shotgun houses, and a modified Creole cottage. Elements of the Greek Revival, Italianate, and Craftsman styles prevail.

ANATOMY OF THE BLOCK: I start at the Laurel end of the block and walk north toward Magazine. I focus my attention on the first house, a double shotgun with a hipped roof, drop lap siding, quoins, and decorative running trim. Like a lot of doubles in our oldest neighborhoods, this one is built at the sidewalk, without a front yard.

A brick church with a trio of arches and tall bell tower comes next. I look for a cornerstone to tell me when it was built and to get an idea of how long the Sixth Baptist Church has occupied the block, but I can't find one. Steps away is a cottage with its front wall right next to the sidewalk. I note the Greek Key door surround and the curvaceous paired brackets and modillions on the entablature, trademarks of the Italianate.

The next house baffles me. Stout, square columns and configuration of the entry doors suggest a twentieth-century Craftsman flavor. But oversized windows on the second floor are out of scale with the openings on the first, and I start to think this is a nineteenth-century house that was remodeled later.

The house to the right is a lovely two-story Italianate double. Identifying features are the segmentally arched windows, transom tops, and door glass. Prominent cornices top every opening, and louvered shutters flank the windows. Elaborate milled brackets add a flourish, complemented by the cast iron railing and fence (likely original).

The Italianate double a few steps closer to Magazine is a camelback. It has the same arched-top windows and transoms as the two-story to its left. Here, the milled brackets are extra large and the scrollwork pierced to create a lacy look.

Two shotguns follow. The first doesn't fool me. Despite its Neoclassical Revival columns, the Greek Key surrounds of the doors and full-length windows tell me this house was built in the nineteenth century, modified in the twentieth. To its right, a Craftsman double shotgun features high-style flared-trim entry assemblies consisting of a door, transom, and sidelights.

Another two-story double follows. It has been altered, but I can picture a second-floor balcony that would have stretched the full width of the house in place of the two separate balconies I see in front of me. The last house on the street is a wide cottage. Also situated at the property line like some others on the block, it achieves privacy by virtue of its solid batten shutters on strap hinges. The Magazine end of the roofline is truncated to conform to the regular shape of the lot.

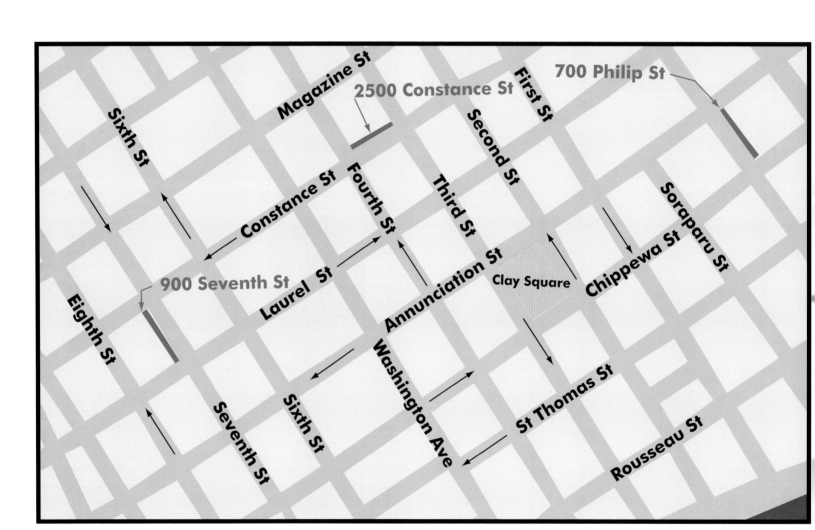

Irish Channel

The Irish Channel was added to the National Register of Historic Places in 1976 and gained protection by the local Historic District Landmarks Commission in the late 1990s. The area is bounded roughly by Magazine Street on the north, Tchoupitoulas Street on the south, Jackson Avenue on the east, and Louisiana Avenue on the west.

In the 1820s, the area was still mostly sugar plantations, but gradually the land was subdivided by its owners and sold for development. According to the National Register's nomination for the Irish Channel, construction in the neighborhood boomed in the era between 1850 and 1890 and much of the architecture standing today dates to that time period.

Shotgun houses, especially doubles, represent the most plentiful house type, in styles ranging from Greek Revival to Italianate to Eastlake to Craftsman. A small number of mid-twentieth-century brick ranch houses or apartment buildings are scattered about.

No one has documented with certainty how the Irish Channel got its name. Although Irish immigrants were plentiful there in the late nineteenth century, German immigrants were also a populous group. The most prominent theory suggests the name appeared after Garden District residents began hiring Irish immigrants as domestic workers and the workers relocated in great numbers to the modest, often two-family dwellings nearby, south of Magazine Street.

2500 block of Constance Street

THE BLOCK: The 2500 block of Constance Street, on the odd-numbered or north side, between Second Street on the east and Third Street on the west. The block is home to Parasol's Bar and Restaurant and the site of New Orleans' best-known St. Patrick's Day celebration. Just one block to the north is Magazine Street, with its shops, coffeehouses, and restaurants; two blocks west is Washington Avenue with a collection of grander homes and immense oaks.

THE HOUSES: Parasol's anchors one end of the block (at Third Street) and a colorful two-story house anchors the other (at Second Street). In between is a collection of shotgun houses—a two-bay single, a sidehall, and four or five doubles.

ANATOMY OF THE BLOCK: Over the past few years, maybe during Hurricane Katrina, Parasol's lost the metal awning that used to wrap around its corner entrance. Nevertheless, I recognize it, a humble white building, with peeling paint and a form that is vaguely Creole cottage-like. I see flags hanging from the eaves, but I'm not sure if they are Irish or Italian, as both St. Patrick's Day and St. Joseph's Day are on the horizon the week I visit.

Next door is a diminutive single shotgun and then a double shotgun with handsome milled brackets and an inviting porch swing. Three or four shotguns follow with a rich variety of details, including arched-top windows, milled brackets, and intricate attic windows. The two-story corner building has a second-floor balcony, turned balusters, and milled brackets. No setback here—its front wall is at the sidewalk. This is a corner storehouse, with its corner entry to what was once a commercial space and a separate entry to the living quarters above. Strings of colored lights stretch from the balcony across the street, reminding me of a street fair I attended long ago in Mexico.

700 block of Philip Street

THE BLOCK: The 700 block of Philip Street, on the odd-numbered or east side of the street, between Annunciation Street on the north and Chippewa Street on the south. Magazine Street's galleries, eateries, and antique stores are just a few blocks to the north, and Jackson Avenue is one block to the east. An elementary school is in the next block.

THE HOUSES: The corner of Annunciation and Philip is anchored by a corner storehouse, a dual-purpose building with a commercial component plus living quarters in the rear. The rest of the block is entirely residential—a collection of five houses including three with Greek Revival details. The houses, unlike the corner storehouse, are set back from the sidewalk.

ANATOMY OF THE BLOCK: A classic corner storehouse with living area attached occupies the corner of Philip and Annunciation. Its commercial days may have passed (I don't think the store is active), but its wonderful corrugated metal awning supported by wood columns wraps around the corner entry, providing shade and shelter from our frequent rains.

The white double next door sits far back from the sidewalk behind a handsome iron fence, the kind of fence that was once ubiquitous in older parts of the city. I note the hipped roof (no front gable), a full-width front porch, box columns, and tall ceilings. Though I can't put my finger on a definite style or date, it has the proportions and form of a late-nineteenth-century house.

When I stand across the street to get a better look at the next houses—a double shotgun on the left and a single on the right—I find I don't have to puzzle about their style or age. Their tall entablatures, parapets, and box columns all suggest they are Greek Revival, one of the older styles found in the Irish Channel.

Before I move on, I realize that both houses also have modillions, small blocks of wood ornamentation, under the cornice—a pair over each column, then singles in between. Could these signal the advent of the Italianate style?

I walk a few paces and realize that neither of the Greek Revival belles is quite as petite as I thought. From another angle, I can see that both have camelbacks and additions at the rear that add volume to the living area.

The same holds true for the blue cottage closer to Chippewa. From the front, it looks like a compact side-gabled building with Greek Key door surrounds—a trademark of the Greek Revival style—a generous front porch and stout box columns. But from the side, it looks much larger, at least four rooms deep with a half-story under the roof. Large walk-through windows balance the tall doorways.

The last house on the block is behind a tall chain-link fence that seems to encircle it and some other buildings, apparently related to a church facing Jackson. The arched-top doors and windows tell me right away that this house is Italianate. It is a very deep shotgun double; I can hardly count how many rooms. I note features including a hipped roof, floor-to-ceiling windows, cornices over the front openings, quoins on the corner board on the front, and handsome milled brackets.

900 block of Seventh Street

THE BLOCK: The 900 block of Seventh Street in the Irish Channel, on the even-numbered or west side of the street, between Constance Street on the north and Laurel Street on the south. As is common in this closely packed neighborhood, homes on this block don't have off-street parking or driveways (though a mid-twentieth-century apartment building does).

THE HOUSES: A collection of nine residential buildings that includes a Creole cottage, five double shotguns, a bungalow, a sidehall shotgun, and a two-story apartment building. There's also a vacant lot.

Some houses are set right on the front property line, at the sidewalk, while others are set back behind modest front yards. As was the practice when the apartment building was constructed, it sits far back on its lot to allow room for parking in front.

ANATOMY OF THE BLOCK: I start my stroll at the corner of Seventh and Laurel and study the block's sole Creole cottage. Though openings on the front have been altered, there is no mistaking it because of its form and roofline—double pitched, steeper toward the ridge and shallower at the eave. And as is typical of Creole cottages, the front wall of the house sits at the sidewalk.

Two double shotguns follow. Based on their proportions and hipped roofs, I think they may have once looked alike. The one on the right, however, still has its original configuration of two front doors and two windows, plus pretty milled brackets under the eave.

I walk a few more steps to the only sidehall shotgun on this side of the street (I notice a few more on the opposite side). Some scholars don't consider sidehalls to be true shotgun houses, because the most strict definition of the shotgun floorplan is a one-room-wide house with a roof ridge perpendicular to the street and a floor plan with rooms en suite, one after another without a hall. Shotgun or not, the sidehall makes the house so much more livable in today's world!

A fine collection of late-nineteenth-century elements gives this sidehall a lot of character. I pick out brackets, cornices over the windows, a recessed entry, drop-lap siding, quoins, a beautifully articulated gable, even an intact iron fence and gate. I choose to ignore the side yard addition that doesn't complement the home's true beauty.

I walk past the vacant lot to the shotgun double that comes next. A thick hedge of jasmine provides a lush green barrier between the shallow front yard and sidewalk. Like the doubles I passed on the Laurel end of the block, this one not only has a hipped roof, but also a full-width front porch and floor-to-ceiling windows.

I have a weakness for Eastlake-style double shotguns like the one I encounter next. This one has it all—the "gingerbread," the turned columns, the spandrels, the frieze—including ornate scrollwork in the gable.

What a jolt, then, to find myself in front of a gigantic swathe of concrete leading to the two-story apartment building. I could go on and on about it, but instead I will say only that such a building is categorized as an "intrusion" in historic districts. Indeed.

I am almost at the corner of Constance where I find two Craftsman-style houses built in the early 1900s. They share features like exposed rafter tails, tapered wood columns atop brick pedestals, and entry doors with sidelights.

The one on the left was built as a double shotgun with a Craftsman facade, but the one on the right is a true Craftsman bungalow. It is a single-family home with an asymmetrical floor plan and arrangement of openings on the facade, likely with a small hallway on the "private" side of the house.

Central City

Central City is a large National Register Historic District about a mile square and comprising nearly 4,000 buildings. The neighborhood is bounded roughly by South Claiborne Avenue on the north, Carondelet Street on the south, the Pontchartrain Expressway on the east, and Louisiana Avenue on the west.

According to the National Register listing from 1982, the development of Central City began in the 1830s when work started on the New Basin Canal and housing was needed for the thousands of immigrant laborers, mostly Irish and German, who worked on the project. Accordingly, the majority of houses built in the area were double shotguns and intended as rental housing. Facades of the shotguns were ornamented to reflect changing fashion, from Italianate to Eastlake in the nineteenth century to Neoclassical and then Craftsman in the twentieth century.

Though not all of Central City was included in the City of Lafayette, the entire neighborhood is included herein for the purpose of simplicity.

2900 block of Baronne Street

THE BLOCK: The 2900 block of Baronne Street, on the odd-numbered or north side of the street, between Sixth Street on the east and Seventh Street on the west. The block features eight houses, four of which are set back from the sidewalk behind iron fences and small front yards. The remaining four, at the Sixth Street end of the block, sit closer to the sidewalk, without front yards.

THE HOUSES: A colorful array of seven double shotguns and one single. The houses closest to Seventh Street are the older ones, based on the nineteenth-century Italianate style of their facades. Of the four closer to Sixth Street, all appear to be from the early twentieth century, two having Neoclassical Revival details and the other two having Craftsman styling.

ANATOMY OF THE BLOCK: The 2900 block of Baronne Street is made up entirely of shotgun houses, without a mix of two-story homes or raised-basement residences. Not only is this condition exemplary of Central City, where shotgun houses of one kind or another compose nearly 85 percent of the residential building stock, but the variety of architectural styles applied to the shotgun frame enlivens the walking experience.

I start at the corner of Baronne and Seventh and walk east toward Sixth. In short order, I encounter a trio of double shotguns adjacent to one another and then a single, each with floor-to-ceiling windows, arched-top windows and transoms, cornices over the openings, and full-width front porches. Identical flourishes in the millwork brackets and equal setbacks behind iron fences tell me these are a quartet of houses that share architectural DNA.

Before long, I am in front of the next two shotguns on the block, both Neoclassical Revival in style, and I note a dramatic change in appearance compared to the first four houses on the block. There are full-width porches, but in lieu of the cantilevered overhangs, milled brackets, and hipped roofs of the Italianate houses, I note front-gabled roofs supported by Corinthian columns. Gable and porch windows feature a complex arrangement of diamond-shaped windowpanes, which contrast with the rectangular simplicity of panes on the older houses. There are no iron fences or front yards here; steps lead straight to the sidewalk.

A few more paces and I admire a duo of Craftsman-style doubles. Color enhances details like the applied wood patterns in the gable, ornaments on the columns, grouped columns atop brick bases, angle brackets under the eaves, and exposed rafter tails.

1200 block of Carondelet Street

THE BLOCK: The 1200 block of Carondelet Street, on the odd-numbered or north side of the street, between Clio and Erato streets. I am visiting Central City's subdistrict known as the Lower St. Charles Avenue area, a square bounded by Oretha Castle Haley Boulevard on the north, St. Charles Avenue on the south, the Pontchartrain Expressway on the east, and Martin Luther King Jr. Boulevard on the west.

The St. Charles Avenue streetcar is just a block away in one direction and Brown's Dairy is equally close in another. Nearby is Crowning Glory Barber Shop & Salon, a coffeehouse, and the Big Top, an art gallery and performance venue.

THE HOUSES: An array of buildings in many styles and sizes, including an immense Greek Revival double townhouse, a colorful sidehall/side-gallery shotgun, a trio of Neoclassical Revival two-story doubles, a mid-twentieth-century apartment building disguised by an artful facade, and a handful of additional buildings.

ANATOMY OF THE BLOCK: I stand in the street taking in the Craftsman-style corner storehouse at the corner of Erato. A trio of Neoclassical Revival houses follows, each with Corinthian columns on the front porch, double doors at the entry, and clipped gables. One of the three still has a low rusticated cement wall serving as a fence at the sidewalk, and I wonder if perhaps all three had something similar at one time.

A few steps farther along I stop to admire a wonderful specimen of a sidehall shotgun with an open gallery on the side. An adventurous paint scheme shows off all the house's features—its drop-lap siding on the front, the decorative verge board cut into fleur de lis shapes on the porch overhang, the milled brackets, the half-glass door.

Next is the 1950s or 1960s apartment complex masquerading as a demure three-bay house. At first glance, it looks like a Creole cottage, roof sloping toward the sidewalk. But then I realize I am looking at a sly front addition that masks a multiunit modern building.

I encounter three more houses before I reach the corner: an immense Greek Revival double-gallery house, a compact two-story house with a classical entablature, and then a Neoclassical Revival single-family home with a balcony.

2400 block of Martin Luther King Jr. Boulevard

THE BLOCK: The 2400 block of Martin Luther King Jr. Boulevard, on the odd-numbered or east side of the street, between Freret Street on the north and LaSalle Street on the south. The block is located in Guste Homes, a subarea of the larger Central City neighborhood. It's hard to picture what this area must have been like 180 years ago when the New Basin Canal was being dug, but the canal was the impetus for the early development of Central City because it created the need for affordable housing for German and Irish immigrants doing the heavy labor. Out of that need grew a neighborhood of predominately modest homes, many of them doubles, and most of which were tenant occupied.

By the early 1960s, the concept of public housing had caught on as a way of addressing urban decay and the lack of affordable housing. Ten square blocks of Central City in this area were cleared in 1963 to make way for the Melpomene Housing Project, which included a twelve-story high-rise building on Simon Bolivar (now senior living) and six low-rise apartment buildings.

Toward the end of the twentieth century, Melpomene Street, the source of the name for the housing project, was renamed Martin Luther King Jr. Boulevard north of St. Charles Avenue. The Melpomene Housing Project itself was renamed for William J. Guste. More important, new ideas had emerged about how to configure and manage public housing. Older models, such as low-rise apartment buildings, were rejected in favor of neighborhoods of one- and two-family residences, detached or semidetached, with private entrances and outdoor spaces.

Plans to convert Guste to new standards began in 2002 and gained momentum in 2004, when several low-rise buildings were demolished and construction began on new residences. Hurricane Katrina slowed the process, but by Thanksgiving of 2007, thirty-two families had returned to the reborn Guste complex.

THE HOUSES: A row of three townhouses having multiple units with private entries. Each exhibits classic styling and proportions without referring to any specific architectural type or style.

ANATOMY OF THE BLOCK: I start at the corner of Freret and walk south toward Simon Bolivar. Soon I realize that the first building on the block is a triplex, three townhouses joined together. The building could have looked blocky, but the designers were clever. They broke up the massing by adding galleries supported by columns on the two end units. Pilasters flank the front doors, giving them prominence. Panels below and cornices above the windows make them seem taller. Cast-iron street lamps provide appealing illumination.

The next building also is a collection of three units, disguised to look like detached residences. The one closest to Freret has an iron balcony on the second level, supported by longer iron brackets. The next begins the transition to a one-story portion, where a gabled roofline extends forward and creates a single-story unit. A building like the one at the Freret corner completes the block: townhouses with galleries at each end of the building and separate entries for the residents.

Uptown

Much of Uptown, which was added to the National Register of Historic Places in 1985, was once Jefferson City, a town which was an incorporated municipal entity of Jefferson Parish as of 1850. Jefferson City was annexed by New Orleans in 1870, just as the City of Lafayette was almost twenty years before it.

Before Jefferson City was established, the land stretching from today's Toledano Street to Audubon Park and from South Claiborne Avenue to the river belonged to seven plantations. Beginning in the early 1800s, plantation owners began subdividing their lands and offering the resulting lots for sale in new "faubourgs" with names like Bouligny, Avart, Rickerville, Hurstville, and more. Gradually the faubourgs coalesced into Jefferson City before it was absorbed by the growing city of New Orleans.

1100 block of General Pershing Street

THE BLOCK: The 1100 block of General Pershing Street, on the odd-numbered or east side of the street, between Coliseum Street on the north and Chestnut Street on the south. The block is located in the Touro-Bouligny neighborhood, an area that was once Faubourg Bouligny, a subdivision carved out of the plantation land owned by Louis Bouligny and laid out by Charles Zimpel in 1833. Zimpel's plan established a boulevard, Napoleon Avenue, which bisected the faubourg into East and West Bouligny. Like all of the other north-south streets of Faubourg Bouligny, General Pershing was originally named by Zimpel to commemorate a major Napoleonic campaign: Berlin. But the name was changed in 1917 both to honor World War I hero Gen. John J. Pershing and likely to express anti-German sentiment after the war.

THE HOUSES: A collection of seven houses in widely varying shapes and styles, dating in age from the late nineteenth century to the first two decades of the twentieth. I spot a center-hall, two double shotguns, a two-story galleried house, a raised basement, and two Craftsman-style houses, one a double and the other a single. All have at least a small front yard, and the center-hall has a beautifully landscaped garden.

ANATOMY OF A BLOCK: The house at the corner of Coliseum is a center-hall having the chaste, clean lines of a Greek Revival house with a few Italianate touches, including modillions in the parapet and paired corbels over the box columns. The house is raised about 3 to 3.5 feet off the ground, not too high to seem unapproachable or too low to detract from its stately grace. The owners have planted a classic garden—boxwoods, oaks, azaleas, and palms—in beds at the edge of the porch and along the wrought iron fence.

The next two houses aren't twins, but they come from the same gene pool. Both shotgun doubles, they exhibit defining elements of the Italianate style in their arched-top windows and door transoms. The one on the left has full-length windows, unlike the shorter windows on the house to its right, but both have handsome milled brackets, quoins, and drop-lap siding.

A lovely two-story house comes next—a sidehall with galleries on both the first and second floors, an entry on the left, and full-length windows next to it and upstairs. Adjacent is a Craftsman double shotgun with a camelback far to the rear. Its strongest feature is the roofline. Instead of forming a pointed triangular shape like most front gables, this one is clipped or flattened, as if the top were shorn off. This roof type is also called a jerkinhead or half-hipped roof. A porch overhang extends out from the front and is supported by flared wood columns resting atop stuccoed pedestals.

The next house is a puzzlement—a raised-basement house, associated with the twentieth century, but having a steeply pitched, side-gabled roofline. The roofline and proportions of the windows on the side make me wonder if the screened-in and arched stucco openings along the front mask an older house.

The house on the Chestnut corner is positively afire with color. It's a cozy little Craftsman cottage painted a brilliant tangerine, with terracotta accents. The owner has adopted a fleur de lis theme and carried it to the extreme. The red medallions that line the bottom edge of the front gable all have gold fleurs de lis in their centers. And the front door? Make sure to take a close look at the metal grille protecting the glass.

1000 block of Marengo Street

THE BLOCK: The 1000 block of Marengo Street in Touro-Bouligny, on the odd-numbered or east side of the street, between Chestnut Street on the north and Camp Street on the south. Many landmarks dot the area, like St. George's Episcopal School, St. Stephen's Church, and the Second District police station. Shops, restaurants, and galleries on Magazine Street offer amenities within walking distance.

THE HOUSES: Eight houses dating from the late nineteenth century to the first couple of decades of the twentieth, including a few double shotguns in varying styles, several single-family homes, and a camelback. Two of the houses are on extra-large lots, providing room for side gardens.

ANATOMY OF THE BLOCK: Starting at the Chestnut corner, I walk toward Magazine. The first few houses, a two story, a double, and a cottage, anchor that end of the block. Next comes a narrow shotgun with a camelback addition. Although the proportions feel right, I get the idea that the house, or some portion of it, may be new.

The house next door is very wide, with six bays across the front. It has a huge side yard and steps of old brick. Full-length windows across the front are shuttered, and the porch is deep, offering shade.

There is nothing subtle about the colors on the bracketed double shotgun next door. The body is painted a pinky-lavender and the trim an intense shade of bluish purple. The colors help bring out the details of the house. The owner of the green Italianate double next door to it has also used color strategically. There is strong contrast between the trim and body color and between the shutter color and the rest. The quoins stand out because their surfaces are painted the body color and their edges the trim color. Here are the old brick steps again, adding another hue to the scheme.

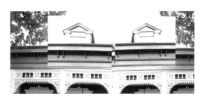

The blue house at the corner of Camp has a cottage roofline with gables on the side and a roof ridge parallel to the street. Dormers accent the roof and a side entry seems to be the main one. Steps used to lead up to the front porch and the gates remain opposite where they used to be, but the owners have chosen to eliminate the front porch as a point of access to the house and now use it as a comfortable sitting area. I notice that the two center openings are pairs of French doors rather than tall windows, and I wonder if they are original or if the owners made the change. Fanciful millwork painted a lacy white against the strong blues of the house, shutters, and ornamental ironwork grace the facade.

1900 block of General Pershing Street

THE BLOCK: The 1900 block of General Pershing Street in the Milan neighborhood of Uptown, on the odd-numbered or east side of the street, between Danneel Street on the north and Dryades Street on the south. Nearby on Napoleon Avenue is Samuel Square, a grassy retreat that mirrors Lawrence Square on the river side of St. Charles Avenue. Just a few blocks away is the historic Stern Tennis Center, which opened in 1897 and is one of the nation's oldest tennis venues.

THE HOUSES: A collection of five late-nineteenth-century houses, perhaps one or two from the very early twentieth century, most with inviting porches. All occupy generously sized lots. The three closest to Danneel appear to have once had identical footprints, though each has evolved a little differently. Closer to Dryades, one house has a porch extending across the front and then down the side. The house on the Dryades corner has a three-sided bay that extends from the front facade at both levels.

ANATOMY OF THE BLOCK: The first thing I notice is how much the three northernmost houses on the block are alike. If you look past differences in columns and the details on the balustrade, all three are tall, two-story houses with steeply pitched roofs and prominent front gables. Each has three openings across the front—a door on the left and two full-length windows on its right—as well as a porch that is situated across the front at both the first and second levels. I am convinced they are contemporaries of one another, even if they were built with slight variations or have evolved differently over time.

The house on the Dryades corner has box columns and a plain picket railing on the second floor. What may have once been a side entry to the house now looks like an entry to a second unit. An addition appears on the right hand side of the house, with 1920s-era casement windows.

Next door, the mocha-colored house offers a surprise—a clipped gable, meaning the gable peak is flat rather than pointed. Instead of box columns and a picket balustrade, it has hefty turned columns and turned balusters. Oversized cutwork brackets extend from the columns, creating interesting arched shapes. But for all the turned millwork and details, the house still resembles its neighbor to the left. It has the same configuration of doors, windows, and porches, plus the same roof pitch.

I recognize the same house form and fanciful millwork, though in a different pattern, at the third house. The fourth may be the grandest house on the block. It occupies an oversized lot and features an exuberant wraparound porch. I study it and try to decide if it was built at the same time as the three I have just visited. It has a similar door and window configuration and a similar steeply pitched roof. If it wasn't built at the same time, it definitely took its cue from its neighbors. It may even have influenced the fifth house, the one on the Dryades Street corner. That one has round, Tuscan columns like those on the fourth house and a wraparound porch.

Palm Terrace

THE BLOCK: Palm Terrace (just one block long), on the odd-numbered or east side of the street, between Carondelet Street on the north and St. Charles Avenue on the south. Two houses in this tiny enclave face Carondelet Street and another faces St. Charles Avenue.

Spain has its Costa del Sol, Greece its Cyclades Islands, and Italy its Amalfi Coast. But New Orleans has its Palm Terrace. Granted, it lacks the limestone cliffs plunging into the emerald sea or citrus groves planted on terraces carved from rock, features that identify its European relatives. Nevertheless, Palm Terrace has its own sense of place.

THE HOUSES: A dozen or so single-story stucco houses with Mediterranean, Moorish, and even Byzantine flavors line both sides of Palm Terrace. All are situated on raised lots and some have stucco retaining walls separating the front terraces from the street. Few are entered from the front. Instead, flights of narrow steps lead up the terraces to side entries. The mix of elements includes stucco walls, flat roofs edged in red tile, loggias with arched openings and twisted columns, small towers (one with a dome), casement windows, and wrought iron.

ANATOMY OF THE BLOCK: Each of the dozen houses is similar to the others in many ways: stucco exteriors, single story, and asymmetrical facades that step back and forward rhythmically. However, none is exactly like the others.

Close to the Carondelet end of the block, the first house has narrow steps ascending on one side and an overall shape that is decidedly cubist. One flat-roofed cube is recessed, the starkness of its facade broken by a gabled bay that extends into the front yard. Another cube, capped with small towerlike details and a fringe of terracotta tiles, steps forward. A white wall retains the front terraced lawn and its aptly placed palm trees.

The next house toward St. Charles is separated from the first by a double driveway, a modern amenity offered when Palm Terrace was developed in the mid-1920s. Flat roofs rimmed in terracotta tiles appear again, but I notice also a tall narrow tower on one end. The house steps back in three planes and a massive pecan tree shelters it from the afternoon sun. Looking down the driveway, I see the side entry is located in an arched portico.

The house closest to the avenue has the same narrow steps to a side entry and the same cubelike elements of varying heights, but its forward-most plane extends almost all the way to the terrace retaining wall and has a gable-ended roof. Set far back on one side is another part of the house, also with a sloped, rather than flat, roof. There is just enough similarity with the others to make this house an unmistakable part of the Palm Terrace family, though it is different enough to make me wonder if it has been modified over the years. Perhaps at one point the owner recognized that the flat roofs so popular in California's bungalow courts weren't suitable for New Orleans monsoons.

800 block of Napoleon Avenue

THE BLOCK: The 800 block of Napoleon Avenue on the even-numbered or west side of the street, between Magazine on the north and Constance on the south. Nearby is Casamento's Restaurant, the oyster emporium.

THE HOUSES: A row of nine houses dating from the end of the nineteenth century to the middle, and possibly late, twentieth century. Types and styles include a ranch house, a sidehall shotgun, a raised-basement house, a camelback shotgun, several Neoclassical Revival doubles, and one house that defies classification. Most have fenced front yards and are shaded by the immense oaks that line this stretch of Napoleon Avenue. Many are decorated for Mardi Gras when I visit.

ANATOMY OF THE BLOCK: It's easy enough to spot the boldest Mardi Gras decorations from a passing car—shiny purple, green, and gold garlands wrapped on stair rails, porches, and even the chains of a porch swing. But until I walk the block and look closely, I don't realize that practically every house on the block is dressed in one kind of Carnival décor or another.

The first house on the block at the corner of Constance is a trim red brick ranch house with a closely clipped lawn. It is a perfect representative of the 1950s or 1960s suburban-style houses that appeared in older neighborhoods when a house was lost or the owner wanted to modernize.

Next door is a sidehall shotgun. I don't think the cast iron columns are original (they likely replaced wood columns), but they are charming. Its terracotta-colored door is adorned with a gold wreath, accented with medallions from Mardi Gras beads. The porch would be a great spot for people- and parade-watching.

The neighboring house is a little newer than the shotgun, likely built in the first quarter of the twentieth century. It's a raised-basement-type house, designed so that the basement is at grade and the living area is above it. Many ground-level basements have been converted to living spaces, but the original design took into account our wet environment. Shimmering bows, striped in the Carnival tricolors, emphasize a garland, and masks hang from the doors.

A robust magnolia tree obscures the view of the shotgun camelback next door, but there is no missing its neighbor to the north. I have watched this house evolve through the years. At one point, I think, it was a single house. Later came additions or the incorporation of a neighboring structure. I note the "fire station" style of the garage doors and the colors. This house is an original.

The two-story double next to it has two views of the passing parade, one from the downstairs porch and one from upstairs. The house itself is handsome, perhaps a 1910-era home with narrow weatherboards, beefy columns, and small windowpanes arranged in patterns in the sash of the downstairs windows. This house and the last three before Magazine share similar elements, all variations on an architectural theme.

4600 block of Coliseum Street

THE BLOCK: The 4600 block of Coliseum Street in the Bouligny neighborhood, on the odd-numbered or north side of the street, between Cadiz Street on the east and Valence Street on the west. The historic St. Peter A.M.E. Church is nearby.

Bouligny was once part of a larger tract of land that Louis Bouligny bought from the Avart family in 1829 with the intention of establishing a sugar plantation. According to the Friends of the Cabildo book on Jefferson City, Bouligny's tract stretched from what is now General Taylor Street on the east to Upperline Street on the west and from the river north toward what is now South Claiborne Avenue. Bouligny sold the portion east of Napoleon Avenue to developers Samuel Kohn and Laurent Millaudon in 1831 and had the western portion subdivided for sale in 1834, after his plantation failed to thrive.

THE HOUSES: A fanciful assortment of five Eastlake houses, including a narrow two-bay single, a double shotgun, and several cottages. All have similar architectural details but none is exactly alike.

ANATOMY OF THE BLOCK: I quickly discover a few key features that tie all five houses together: the steeply pitched roofs, the abundant and varied decorative millwork, and the turned columns. All are raised a good bit above the ground, too. On the narrow single closest to the corner of Valence Street, I note an especially elaborate gable, having a large center window flanked by two smaller windows inset with stained glass. Frilly scrollwork fills in between the window edges and the gable ends. Accented with blue paint, these elements make for the most striking gable on the block.

Next door is a double. Its front doors are unusual, consisting of half glass with four square inset panels on the bottom, just like the door on the house with blue accents. The turned columns are different, though. This is where I first see the cubelike motif midway up the column and the millwork element that resembles a bonnet over the windows. Atop the columns is an elaborate frieze with piercework and spandrels, a motif that will appear repeatedly as I proceed down the block. The defining feature here? It must be gable-ended extensions of the porch overhang marking the locations of the entry doors.

Now I am in front of a yellow house with red trim. The columns, the frieze, the spandrels are all here, but instead of extending forward, the entry is recessed so that the front porch wraps down one side a short distance leading to the door. This is the only house on the block with a decorative railing between the columns, and it's a railing that uses spindles and piercework like those in the frieze above to create a singular pattern.

The house adjacent has the same columns and frieze I noted before, but now I see a bay on the left that extends forward from the main body of the house. There is no doubt that the front porch used to extend forward more than it does now, allowing the front two columns to rest on it rather than on stucco bases on the ground.

At the last house, I see the bay again but configured a little differently. The other elements are here, too—the bonnets, turned columns, and frieze—and the porch appears to be in its original condition. Unlike the others, though, this house has a generous side yard, which makes it possible to appreciate from additional angles.

4900 block of Danneel Street

THE BLOCK: The 4900 block of Danneel Street, on the odd-numbered or north side of the street, between Upperline on the east and Robert on the west in Uptown's Freret neighborhood. With its monthly arts market, coffee house, boxing gym, garden center, hardware store, and restaurants, Freret Street has come into its own as the neighborhood's "Main Street."

THE HOUSES: Five Arts and Crafts-style homes, including a two-story single-family residence and four shotgun doubles. Although the large single-family home sits back from the sidewalk, the doubles are situated much closer. All houses have front porches, desirable amenities for talking with neighbors and keeping up with happenings on the block.

ANATOMY OF THE BLOCK: The house closest to the corner of Robert Street is the block's only two-story house and, as far as I can tell, its only single-family residence. It has porches the width of the house

both upstairs and down, and I notice that the front-facing gable is stucco rather than wood, with a double attic window. The asymmetry of the arrangements of "lights" or panes is a hallmark of the Craftsman style, one I will see again and again as I make my way down the block.

Before I move on, the first-floor porch columns and beams atop them attract my attention. Atop each of the columns rest two beams that run parallel to the facade of the house. On top of the two beams rest three pairs of similar beams installed perpendicular to the facade. The lower and upper sets cross one another atop the two columns and in the center, creating a complex and high-style Craftsman facade.

I find more evidence of superior design intent on the house next door. Most striking is its elaborate gable, having an angle bracket at the peak and a stuccoed area above a band of wood siding. Centered in the wood siding band

are two fifteen-light attic windows. Just below the band of siding, a wide band of flat boards or fascia separates the gable from the stucco entablature resting on a trio of short wood columns on brick bases.

Like many Craftsman-style houses, this one has an entry assembly consisting of a door in the middle, sidelights on either side of the door, and a transom across the top. Not so common is the care that was taken to tie the design of these features in with the design framework established in the gable. Although the house next door is a twin, there aren't many transoms with twenty small, square panes or sidelights with the complex asymmetrical configuration of the ones I see before me.

A few paces farther along, I come upon a house following the same patterns but applying the elements a little differently. Here, for instance, the front-facing gable is present only on the left side of the double and the roof over the right half is hipped. The entry

assemblies have the multipaned transoms and sidelights I saw on the two previous houses, but these go a step further because the trim surrounding them isn't an even width from top to bottom; the width varies. Instead of a trio of plain columns atop each brick pedestal, there is just one column, heftier and with millwork at the top.

The house at Danneel and Upperline has an elaborate gable like the ones I saw on the first two doubles, but here it is even more highly stylized. It has the entry door, sidelight, and transom assembly, too. This assembly is the most complex on the block—the side trim flares outward from top to bottom and glass panes in the door, sidelights, and transom are intricately arranged.

2200 block of Valence Street

THE BLOCK: The 2200 block of Valence Street, on the odd-numbered or east side of the street, bounded by South Liberty on the north and Loyola on the south. The Freret Street Market operates monthly nearby, and in the 2300 block is the Samuel J. Green Charter School. The school's curriculum integrates lessons from its Edible Schoolyard, an organic garden and teaching tool based on the California prototype pioneered by Chef Alice Waters and her Chez Panisse Foundation. Via their involvement with the garden and its products, students learn about cultural traditions involving food, seasonal changes in the environment, stewardship of the earth, nutrition, health, and more.

THE HOUSES: A delectable array of shotgun houses, including a newish single and eight doubles, two of which are in the Neoclassical Revival style and six in the Italianate-bracketed style. Most of the latter have been repainted recently, bringing the block to life with color.

ANATOMY OF THE BLOCK: The house closest to South Liberty Street is a modest white house in the single-shotgun tradition—long and narrow with a side gallery. Next to it, two Neoclassical Revival shotgun doubles stand side by side. Both are set back from the sidewalk a bit and are raised with porches across the fronts. The one on the left still has its Tuscan columns (replaced on the house to the right with wrought iron), and both have dormers that extend forward from the roof ridge. On the white house, I see that the original dormer window, or half of it, remains in place, its iridescent stained glass sparkling in the sun.

The six bracketed doubles that follow could be mistaken easily for cookie cutter, but a keen house sleuth will note the differences that make for a fascinating streetscape even without their rich palette of colors.

All six sit right on the sidewalk, stoops reaching forward. All but one have hipped roofs; the exception has a gable-fronted roof and deeper overhang. Though the pattern sometimes varies, all of these doubles have facades with doors on the outside and windows in the center. Every one, except the house with the red doors close to Loyola, has drop-lap siding and a panel of quoins at the edge.

When I look more carefully, I see that the brackets are the key to deciphering the differences between the houses. The bracket design is identical on the first three houses I pass. However, the next house interrupts the pattern. It's the nonconformist of the group anyway, with its gable-front roof and floor-to-ceiling windows in lieu of shorter ones. The brackets on this house are different from those on the first three bracketed houses and also from the two houses that follow. They are much longer than elsewhere to fit the deeper soffit, and the pattern is entirely different. Are the differences here the result of a creative renovator or are the features original?

At the Loyola end of the block are two doubles that no doubt looked alike before someone altered the one on the left. Seeing the beauty of the house at the corner, I wonder if pulling back the vinyl siding on its neighbor would reveal the same architectural richness.

1500 block of Dufossat Street

THE BLOCK: The 1500 block of Dufossat Street, on the odd-numbered or east side of the street, between Atlanta Street on the north and Pitt Street on the south, in the Faubourg Avart area of Uptown. St. Charles Avenue and its streetcars are just a block away, as is the historic Latter Branch Public Library, formerly the home of a silent film star. Nearby, Prytania Street's commercial district offers numerous amenities, including restaurants, exercise studios, a grocer, an ice cream parlor, and vendors of wine and cheese.

THE HOUSES: Five large two-story houses from the twentieth century, situated on generous lots. Although each is different, four of them fit roughly in the Neoclassical Revival-style category. Just one house, at the corner of Pitt, might be considered as the slightly earlier style of Queen Anne.

ANATOMY OF THE BLOCK: I start at the corner of Dufossat and Atlanta at a two-story house painted a rich caramel with blue shutters. It has an inviting front porch and a wealth of architectural details. When I visit, the home's architectural character is overshadowed by the ebullient holiday display the owners stage every year. The theme is bears: polar bears with balls; leafy bear topiaries; white, furry bears dressed for a marching band; bears on rocking horses; bears on the lawn; bears on the front porch; and bears in all the windows.

I move on, not because I've had enough of bears but because the rest of the block has its own charms. The house next to the bear house has a handsome entry porch, its roof supported by paired columns. Above it, walk-through windows in the bay allow access to the porch. The third house has a deep porch extending across the entire front and wrapping around one side. Steeply pitched gables and a tall, narrow dormer add interest to the roofline and feature gable windows in three distinct designs.

The fourth house shares a lot of features with its neighbor on the left, especially the wide front porch and the two-story bay on the right side. Unlike the other houses on the block, its front yard is fenced, and I spot a custom iron pattern that resembles reeds or bull rushes.

The multifamily home at the corner of Pitt is shaded by a large oak, which makes it hard to see all of its features. I note turned wood columns and spandrels on the ground level and a distinctive recessed porch with turned balusters on the second floor. Roof dormers here are highly unusual. Instead of extending out from the pitch of the roof, these are recessed into the attic.

600 block of Jefferson Avenue

THE BLOCK: The 600 block of Jefferson Avenue, on the even-numbered or west side of the street, between Laurel Street on the north and Annunciation Street on the south. The block is located in what was once Faubourg Rickerville, a subdivision on the upriver edge of Jefferson City and bounded by what today is South Claiborne Avenue on the north, the Mississippi River on the south, Valmont Street on the east, and Joseph Street on the west. A marker on the neutral ground at the corner of Jefferson and Magazine streets notes the area's founding and history.

THE HOUSES: Six houses, including five Eastlake shotguns, both doubles and singles, and a Craftsman double.

ANATOMY OF THE BLOCK: An Arts and Crafts double stands at the corner of Jefferson and Annunciation, where I start my walk. It has clusters of three wood box columns at each corner, set atop a stucco half-column. Exposed rafter tails and post brackets under the eaves put this house solidly in the early-twentieth-century Craftsman category.

Once I pass this house, the styling is totally different. I am in the midst of a cadre of houses in the Eastlake style, popular at the end of the nineteenth century. The first of the Eastlake beauties is a colorful double shotgun converted to a single, having a host of features that set the tone for the rest of the block. I note fancifully turned columns, accented with bands of color, a three-part gable window in stained glass surrounded by shingles, a spindle frieze between the column tops, milled spandrels, floor-to-ceiling windows with cornices above, and a half-glass front door.

Next door to the double-turned-single is a sidehall shotgun with a wider rear portion. It shares the Eastlake style and many of the same features of its neighbor, but I notice that its millwork isn't identical to that on its neighbor to the left. The spindles have a different form, the columns have a different shape, and the spandrels have a different pattern. The gable window is round, unlike the three-part stained-glass window next door.

Another sidehall follows, and its details appear to be identical to the first, except for the rear portion. On this one, the rear wing is side gabled. The fifth house is a double shotgun with candy-apple red doors. I notice that this house, as well as the one to its right, has the same columns, spandrels, frieze, and gable windows as the double near the other end of the block and conclude that they were likely built at the same time.

When I look at the sixth and last house on the block, I fantasize about how I would paint it. A little sanding and a color or two of well-placed paint would do wonders here, but even without paint, the house is a treasure.

5400 block of Coliseum Street

THE BLOCK: The 5400 block of Coliseum Street on the odd-numbered or north side of the street, between Jefferson Avenue on the east and Octavia Street on the west. The block is located in what was Rickerville, a subdivision carved from land owned by the Ricker family and others according to a plan devised by Benjamin Buisson and W. T. Thompson in the late 1840s. Peters Avenue—now Jefferson—was established as the new subdivision's primary thoroughfare and the streets flanking it were named for Leontine and Octavine Ricker, two of the owners of the original plantation. Today, the schoolyard of Benjamin Franklin Elementary Mathematics and Science School sits across the street from the block.

THE HOUSES: A trio of houses of varying size, type, and style, including two sidehall shotguns and a highly ornamental raised house in the Eastlake style, bordering on the Queen Anne.

ANATOMY OF THE BLOCK: The sidehall shotgun at the corner of Coliseum and Octavia shares some of the millwork vocabulary of the pink Eastlake/Queen Anne house farther down the block. I see turned columns, piercework panels in the spindle frieze, quoins, louvered shutters, and drop-lap siding. The very steeply pitched roof forms a forward-facing gable, filled with fish-scale shingles and a stained-glass window topped with a millwork flourish. Everything except for window and door casings and a trim board on the gable is painted one color—a muted gray green. The color scheme demands that you stop and take your time if you want to appreciate the home's fine details.

A few steps closer to Jefferson is a sidehall shotgun, also with a steeply pitched roof. Though this house has no front porch (save for a red brick stoop), turned columns, or spindle course like the house to its left, there are just enough similarities to make me wonder if the two houses might have looked alike at one point. The roof pitch, the drop-lap siding, and the quoins all are similar to those on the neighbor. I notice that even the style of the shutter looks the same. True, the gable has siding rather than shingles and a half-round rather than rectangular attic window, so I make a mental note to check the Sanborn Fire Insurance Maps—the ones that show the footprint of buildings when the maps were made—from the 1890s and early 1900s to determine if both houses appeared at the same time.

Now I reach the pink diva on the block. It is fairly wide but appears even larger because of the galleries that extend across the front and down both sides and because it is raised high off the ground. All manner of fanciful millwork is present, complemented by a square porch bay on the left and a turretlike one on the right. The asymmetry adds to the appeal.

1600 block of Octavia Street

THE BLOCK: The 1600 block of Octavia Street on the odd-numbered or east side of the street, between Danneel Street on the north and St. Charles Avenue on the south. The block is situated in Hurstville, a neighborhood that was a plantation, then a faubourg, and then part of Jefferson City before being annexed to New Orleans in 1870.

The block faces Danneel Park, identified by a stone obelisk at its St. Charles Avenue end as "Danneel Place," established in memory of Hermann Danneel and his wife in 1906. The Danneel family owned a large home on the site, which was donated to the city by the Danneels' sons after their death for use as a public park. Generations of New Orleans families have made Danneel Park the site of picnics, birthday parties, and play dates.

THE HOUSES: Six elegant houses, several of them very large, and ranging in age from mid-nineteenth century to early twentieth century. Several center-hall houses are present, as is a two-story stucco house with a Craftsman flair. Most occupy extra large lots.

ANATOMY OF THE BLOCK: The pale lavender stucco building at the corner of Danneel and Octavia is two stories tall with an entry porch projecting from the facade. I notice a few features that suggest the Craftsman style—the multipaned top sash over the single-paned bottom, the stout columns on the entry porch and its front-gabled roof with exposed rafter tails.

Next door stands a center-hall house with so much variety that I study it for some time. This is not a traditional center-hall, in the style of a mid-nineteenth-century house, where there is a porch across the full width of the house. Here, the center doorway is flanked on the left by a bay that projects forward, reducing the width of the front porch.

The porch extends across the remainder of the front, then down the right side. The bay has a front-gabled roof, a band of shingles at the top of the wall and spandrels in the gable that connect the walls of the bay to the roof overhang. On the porches, turned columns support the roof and an open frieze with spindles fills in between the columns. Above, a steep roof features a remarkable dormer with an oversized roof and siding that wraps the corners rather than ending in a miter or edge board.

The third house is a two-story in shining white with pale blue shutters. Here the entry is on the left side of the house with a semihexagonal bay in the center. Sunburst-style brackets connect the walls of the bay to its gable-fronted roof, much as they do on the house to the left.

Closer to St. Charles Avenue is another center-hall with a shallow bay to the right of the front door but a full-width porch. The railing is cast iron in an oak-leaf pattern, and the columns are rounded rather than turned. Its most striking feature is the dormer, with its sunburst-patterned gable, round columns supporting its roof, and what looks like a small balcony.

I realize when I reach the fifth house on the block that it can be classified as a center-hall too. It is more intimate in scale than the others but has a porch across part of the front and a bay—this time with an almost conical roofline—to the left of the front door. The roof over the porch is front gabled and supported by turned columns dressed up with spandrels.

The last house on the block is a two-story center-hall of grand proportions. I read somewhere once that this house used to face St. Charles Avenue and had a gallery across the full width of the front at the second level. The front door is recessed in an entry flanked by pilasters and a gentle arch, in the Italianate style.

5900 block of Laurel Street

THE BLOCK: The 5900 block of Laurel Street, on the odd-numbered or north side of the street, between Eleonore Street on the east and State Street on the west. Both sides of the street face Gilmore Park, a long, narrow green space with a winding path and welcoming benches that continues on west of State Street and in front of houses in the 6000 block of Laurel Street. Gilmore Park was once a public market, but it was turned into a park in 1903.

THE HOUSES: Thirteen houses face the park on the north side, most of them shotguns. But nonshotguns include a two-story corner storehouse on the corner of State, a ranch house next to it, and another two-story in the middle of the block.

ANATOMY OF THE BLOCK: The building at the corner of State and Laurel is called a corner storehouse, owing to the fact that it was designed to provide work space at the ground level and residential space above. Customers would enter the shop through the corner entry, but family and guests would enter a private side door leading straight up to the family's living quarters. This building was "mixed use" long before the zoning designation was invented.

A jazzy little ranch house next door has Bahama shutters and a vintage Thunderbird in the driveway to distinguish it. The owners have imbued it with an expressive personality, which complements the older, fancier houses on the block.

Now I have reached the first shotgun of ten on this long block. It is an Eastlake sidehall single with a huge side yard and a wider wing at the rear. The house that follows is also in the Eastlake style, with turned columns and a fancy gable. This one, though, is a double shotgun that has been converted to a single, a practice prevalent in older neighborhoods.

Another Eastlake shotgun, the fifth house on the block, retains its double entries, suggesting it also retains its original floor plan and houses two families. Here, the tops of the cornices over the floor-to-ceiling windows wear frilly scalloped millwork, rather like tiaras. Next door is a white shotgun with green awnings, a perfect example of how the facades of shotgun houses took on whatever style was in vogue when they were built. The shotgun houses I passed previously on the block were all in the millwork-obsessed Eastlake style of the late nineteenth century, but this one is in the Arts and Crafts style popular several decades after its neighbors were built.

Mid-block is a two-story family home, which serves as a vertical break between the shotgun houses to its right and left. Details like the wood columns atop masonry pedestals and the deep eave in the gabled front belong in the Craftsman category, suggesting it may have been built about the same time as the house to its left. On the other hand, it may not be an old house at all, but a newer one built in a vintage style.

And now for the crescendo—six shotguns in an unbroken row, each different from the next. The first is a sidehall shotgun with a camelback and angle brackets under the eave of the hipped roof. Then a trio of doubles (two of them converted to singles) with elaborate millwork brackets instead of the turned columns of the Eastlake houses closer to State.

A camelback double follows, much bigger than is evident at first because the mass of the camelback is recessed far back from the sidewalk. The last house is a double shotgun in the Neoclassical Revival style, popular in the early twentieth century. The front gable on the house is clipped, meaning it is flat rather than pointed on top, and is embellished with modillions in its eaves.

1500 block of Calhoun Street

THE BLOCK: The 1500 block of Calhoun Street, on the odd-numbered or east side of the street, between St. Charles Avenue on the north and Benjamin Street on the south. The block is in the University Section of Uptown in an area once called Burtheville.

According to the Friends of the Cabildo volume on the architecture of the University Section, Burtheville was subdivided in 1854 from a narrow sliver of land owned by Dominique Francois Burthe and auctioned off in 1867. It compromised "sixty-nine squares of ground subdivided into fourteen hundred and ninety two lots" and was "the last of the Uptown faubourgs to be subdivided and laid out in streets and squares." At the time of the auction, Burtheville was still largely undeveloped, but that changed by the 1880s.

Today, this area close to Audubon Park is the location of some of Uptown's most recognized landmarks: Tulane University, Loyola University, Holy Name of Jesus Church, and Temple Sinai.

THE HOUSES: Eight late-nineteenth-century homes, including three two-story traditional homes, three Eastlake camelbacks, and two Neoclassical Revival cottages.

ANATOMY OF THE BLOCK: I start at the corner of St. Charles Avenue and walk south toward the river, passing the first two houses on the block. I stop at the third one—a warm yellow confection with white trim and leaf-green shutters. The form of the main part of the house is similar to that of a sidehall shotgun—with a front door off to the left side and two full-length windows on the porch. A wing, possibly a later addition, extends off the left side of the house.

The Neoclassical Revival style of the house shines in its Tuscan columns, diamond-patterned windowpanes, gable window, and casement windows in the side wing. The gable detailing is especially engaging. The applied wood strips in a grid pattern and other applied decoration on the rake boards look as much like icing on a cookie as molding on a house.

The next house is similar in terms of the gable over the bay. It has more of the millwork I liked next door. But this house is a late-nineteenth- or very early-twentieth-century version of a center-hall. The front door is located in the middle, between a protruding bay on the left and full-length windows on the right. There's a special visual reward on the river side gable of the house for anyone walking in my footsteps. I won't tell you what it is; you'll have to see for yourself.

The next three houses are Eastlake camelbacks, a white sidehall first, then two doubles. Many elements unite them stylistically, including the open frieze with spindles across the front, milled brackets, balustrades on the porches, quoins on the corner boards, and semicircular windows in the gables. But one common element that is possible to miss is the iron fence and gate leading to each set of steps. Same pattern, same gates, and no fences between the properties are more evidence these houses were built at the same time.

A two-story house is the last on the block at the corner of Benjamin Street. It's laid out in a three-bay configuration—door and two windows on the first floor—suggesting the presence of a sidehall and stairs to the second level. The roof is hipped but very steep and there is a band of decorative millwork at the top of the facade, just under the eave. I spend some time looking at its lush side garden, but I move along to make it home before dark.

500 block of Webster Street

THE BLOCK: The 500 block of Webster Street, on the even-numbered or west side of the street, between Patton Street on the north and Laurel Street on the south. The block is located in the Uptown Historic District in an area once known as Bloomingdale before its incorporation into New Orleans. Audubon Park is just a few blocks away.

THE HOUSES: A varied assortment of shotgun houses (some converted to singles). No two houses are alike or have quite the same form. There is no common setback from the sidewalk, no uniformity of fencing or gardens. Yet the collection works, both individually and as a whole.

ANATOMY OF THE BLOCK: I start my walk near the corner of Laurel and study the first house I encounter. It is a three-bay shotgun with turned columns and an array of Eastlake millwork. I see that the house has a crisp front garden featuring creeping jasmine ground cover and a ponytail fern.

As I continue, I am shaded by a river birch planted between the sidewalk and the street, and I note that the peeling bark adds texture to the trunks.

Next door, a Neoclassical Revival house has fancy Corinthian columns, tapered, round columns with elaborate capitals at the top. Diamond-patterned windowpanes fill the top sash of each window on the front porch, and a Palladian attic window fills in the front gable. I remind myself to always look up to make sure I don't miss any details.

As I walk on toward Patton Street, I notice that the third house on the block, a shotgun double, shields its eyes from the sun with one of those metal awnings I see so often in our neighborhoods. I lean against the gate and peek under the awning. Sure enough, its original architectural details are still there, just concealed. The lush garden on one side suggests perhaps that the owner lives on that side and a tenant on the other.

I continue to a two-bay shotgun single with a side addition. It has box columns instead of Corinthian ones like those on its next-door neighbor or turned columns of other houses behind me. I note the full-length, shuttered windows on the front porch, where I can picture the owners enjoying the afternoon at a table with chairs.

The fifth house looks like a double converted to a single. I see yet a fourth column type on this house, chamfered with applied wood decorations suggestive of the Craftsman style. This house sits back from the sidewalk a little more than the others, and then I notice that none of the fronts of the houses on this block align exactly, creating a rhythm that depends less on repetition than on syncopation.

2600 block of Jefferson Avenue

THE BLOCK: The 2600 block of Jefferson Avenue, on the odd-numbered or east side of the street, between Willow Street on the north and Clara Street on the south. The block is located in a part of the Uptown Historic District once known as Rickerville, a community that was subdivided for development in the 1840s and stretched from South Claiborne Avenue to the river and from Valmont Street to Joseph Street.

THE HOUSES: Closest to Willow, there's a brick ranch house and two 1930s-era stucco duplexes. Closer to Clara, three two-story houses have proportions suggesting they were once raised-basement, Craftsman houses that were modified so that the ground-level basement became the first floor of the living area.

One of the houses is detached from its foundation, raised up in the air and sitting on stout piles of wood cribbing. The sight of a house like this one being elevated has been common since Hurricane Katrina, as homeowners have scrambled to mitigate the potential for flooding and qualify for affordable flood insurance. But as the five-year anniversary of the storm approaches, there are fewer opportunities to study the work in progress, so I can't resist taking a closer look.

ANATOMY OF THE BLOCK: I start at the corner of Jefferson and Willow and walk toward Clara, passing the nicely landscaped brick ranch at the corner. I move on immediately to study the two stucco duplexes to its right.

From the looks of the almost horizontal eaves of the house on the left and the gable-ended roof with brackets of the house on the right, I can tell they were likely built in the 1920s or 1930s in the Mediterranean Revival and Craftsman styles, respectively. On each house, doors on the right side offer access to stairs to the second-floor unit, while entry to the first-floor unit is gained from the porch. I pause, trying to analyze why the duplexes appear so tall, and then I get it. Each has a ground-level basement in addition to the two stories of living space.

Up-down duplexes like these are less common in New Orleans than side-by-side doubles. In many ways, though, the up-down arrangement is superior to the side-by-side, for each unit is full width, rather than half, allowing for more gracious floor plans and privacy afforded by hallways.

I continue walking toward Clara and stop at a two-story Craftsman house set at grade. Its roofline is distinctive. A front-facing gable over the main body of the house both pierces and intersects the side-gabled roofline over the front rooms. Most striking, though, is what I notice about the house's proportions and the clues they offer to its past. It appears as though the ceiling height on the ground level is lower than that on the upper level of the house. The same holds true for the green Colonial Revival adjacent (on cribbing) and the house at the corner of Clara.

For most houses, ceiling height on the first floor is equal to or greater than that on the second, so this inverse proportion gets me thinking. I wonder if the first floors of all three might have once been ground-level basements with low ceilings that were later recruited into serving as the ground floor and entry level of each house.

If so, this approach represents a departure from the more common ways in which ground-level basements—originally intended as flood mitigation elements—are incorporated into living spaces. Most often, owners either finish them out and rent them as apartments or convert them to dens or rec rooms downstairs from the primary living space. It's unusual to see the space become what it appears to be here—the first floor of a large family home.

2700 block of Joseph Street

THE BLOCK: The 2700 block of Joseph Street, on the odd-numbered or east side of the street, between Story Street on the north and Cucullu Street (previously Delord) on the south. Houses on the block benefit from deep front lawns and wide lots plus a view of a magnificent row of oaks along Cucullu Street at the rear of the Eleanor McMain School, home of the Mighty Mustangs and an Art Deco masterpiece in its own right.

THE HOUSES: Seven cottages built sometime between the 1920s and 1930s, each in a different style and configuration. The houses appear modest from the front, but a view down the sides contradicts that impression. Like many homes of the era, these were built with the automobile in mind, and so each has a driveway.

ANATOMY OF THE BLOCK: What makes the 2700 block of Joseph Street so appealing is the variety of rooflines, porches, and architectural elements incorporated into the 1930s-style cottages on the street. Take the house at the corner of Joseph and Story. It has a front-facing gable roofline, but side projections and a clever bay in front animate the facade. Front steps lead to a screened-in porch, a pleasant transition from the outside world to the private enclave.

The front-facing gable theme carries through to the blue house adjacent, where it's found in triplicates, with each portion of the house widening slightly and stepping back a little bit from the portion in front of it. The forward-most facade holds a trio of casement windows with paneled bottoms; the portion behind it holds the entry door; and the third gabled portion—wider still and recessed farther—is a side entrance.

A gabled front is prominent on the ochre-colored stucco house next door. Present on the right side of the front, the gable appears above a shallow bay and features Tudor Revival-style millwork. Below it, windows in the bay center on the gable peak and help anchor the soaring element above.

On the fourth house, I suspect that the columns and connecting arches on its facade and side wings may have once ringed open porches, now enclosed for living space. What hasn't changed, though, is the interesting roofline, hipped over the central wing, then side-gabled over the main body of the house. The semicircular millwork sunburst in the center of the front-hipped roof helps break up the visual mass of the roof and guides attention to the entry.

As I move on, I notice that the double gables on the fifth house are especially prominent, due in part to the fact that they are lighter in color than the body of the house and sided in wood rather than stucco. With body, trim, and gables painted in creamy, neutral tones, the vivid blue of the front door makes a strong statement.

The Colonial Revival double next door has the simplest roofline on the block when observed from the front only—a side-gabled roof with a forward extension supported by columns to shade the front porch. But when I check out the sides, I see that wings, bays and connectors more than double the volume of the house. If I didn't already believe it, the houses on this block would convert me to the philosophy that you can't take things at face value.

Now I am in front of the English cottage-inspired house at the corner of Joseph and Cucullu. Its tall, steeply pitched gables, one with an upward flip at the right eave, define the home's personality and mark the location of the recessed entry. The main body of the house rises behind the gables and a smaller wing is recessed on the left side, adding volume to the home. Tudor Revival millwork in the gables makes them still more pronounced.

Carrollton

Carrollton is a vast historic district added to the National Register of Historic Places in 1987 and bounded roughly by Earhart Boulevard on the north, the Mississippi River on the south, Broadway (officially Lowerline Street) on the east, and the Orleans-Jefferson Parish line on the west. Originally a town in its own right, Carrollton was the seat of government for Jefferson Parish, where development in the area was spurred by the establishment of the New Orleans and Carrollton Railroad in 1836 followed by the Jefferson and Lake Pontchartrain Railroad in 1851. Carrollton was annexed by New Orleans in 1874, just a few years after Jefferson City and Algiers.

The Carrollton district encompasses many communities, including Black Pearl, Carrollton-Riverbend, Central Carrollton, Fontainebleau, Hollygrove, Maple Area, Marlyville, and Northwest Carrollton.

Oak Street, now a "Main Street" area, serves as Carrollton's commercial core and Carrollton Avenue as its residential boulevard. Verdant Palmer Park provides a respite and a venue for the monthly arts market.

A few of the blocks profiled in this chapter fall outside of the official boundaries of the Carrollton district but are considered part of it by the City Planning Commission.

9200 Palm St

8900 Edinburgh St

Palm St

Edinburgh St

Apricot St

Earhart Expwy

S Claiborne Ave

8200 Apricot St

Fontainebleau Dr

2300 Dublin St

Trianon Plaza

42-56
Fontainebleau Dr

Dublin St

S Carrollton Ave

Willow St

8300 Willow St

2000 Burdette St

Burdette St

1000 Dublin St

7500 Zimpel St

Zimpel St

Hampson St

7800 Pearl St

7600 St Charles Ave

7300 Hampson St

St Charles Ave

Pearl St

7300 block of Hampson Street

THE BLOCK: The 7300 block of Hampson Street, on the odd-numbered or north side of the street, between Pine Street on the east and Lowerline Street on the west. The block is just a bit off Broadway with its university-related residences and businesses. And though it falls within the generally accepted boundaries of the Carrollton neighborhood (west of Broadway), it is technically in the westernmost sliver of Uptown, once known as Greenville.

THE HOUSES: Three large early-twentieth-century houses situated on even larger lots, each beautifully landscaped and filled with graceful oaks, blooming roses, and chaste boxwood hedges.

ANATOMY OF THE BLOCK: I start at the corner of Lowerline and Hampson and walk east toward Pine. First, I stand across the street so I can take in the entire streetscape, and then I move to the sidewalk in front of the houses to enjoy their details.

The first house is a two-story with a front porch that wraps the corner and continues down the right side on both the first and second floors. Its most striking feature is a prominent gable inset with paired windows and trimmed with a distinctive rake board in an undulating pattern accented by a circular cutout. A similar curvy pattern with cutout appears in the spandrels at the top of the columns on the first floor.

On the left side of the front porch, a swing offers a spot to while away an afternoon in the shade, compliments of an oak tree at the corner. The porch on the right side of the house is more private than the front. It is screened from the street by a trio of shutters installed between a pair of columns. Looking back at the house from in front of the second house on the block, I notice for the first time gables on the side elevation, one over a bay and the other over a side wing. Both have the same frilly treatment as the front gable.

The yellow house next door is set far back from the sidewalk, farther than either of the two houses that flank it. Called upon to categorize this house by style, I'd say Colonial Revival, owing to the simplicity of the design and the characteristic front door with sidelights and arched-top transom.

Landscaping here is structured and formal, suiting the geometry of the house. A low row of boxwoods lines the brick pathway to the front door and the sidewalk. Beyond the low hedge, a carpet of grass stretches to the front porch, which is lined with Tuscan columns.

The third house on the block is extraordinarily wide, raised at least six feet off the ground, and features an immense gable. Here the deep front porch wraps around both sides, screened on the left and open on the right. Four white rocking chairs line up on the front porch, ready for the homeowners to observe the action on the street.

I consider the massive gable on this house and try to understand why it dominates the composition, especially when compared to the gable of the first house on the block. I conclude it is in fact wider because it extends past the sides of the house and over a few feet of the side porches. Then there is the matter of proportions. The gable on this house rests atop a single level of living space having lower ceilings than on the first house, making it appear even larger than it really is.

7600 block of St. Charles Avenue

THE BLOCK: The 7600 block of St. Charles Avenue, on the odd-numbered or north side of the street, between Hillary Street on the east and Adams Street on the west. A few blocks away in one direction are the restaurants and shops of Maple Street. Nearby in another direction are popular venues in Riverbend and along Oak Street.

THE HOUSES: Four very large houses on expansive lots, each with a generous front porch and suited for watching the Phunny Phorty Phellows, who parade by streetcar each year on Twelfth Night, January 6. No other parades use the avenue in this location.

ANATOMY OF THE BLOCK: The houses on the block are so large that I have to stand on the neutral ground to take them in. One is set back rather far from the street, but the others are less recessed. All have multiple levels, at least two stories each and more like three.

I start at the corner of Adams Street and walk east, stopping first at a two-story house with up/down porches and a bay on the left side. Tuscan columns support the porch roof and glass doors offer entry to the inside. Residents of every house on the block, including this one, still have their holiday decorations up when I visit in early January. Perhaps, like me, they are waiting for Twelfth Night to take them down.

A few more steps and I get a good look at a raised stucco house with dramatic stairs. Lots of Neoclassical Revival elements make the facade interesting—the grouped and rounded columns, the diamond-patterned panes in many of the windows. I also detect a hint of a Craftsman flavor in the deep eaves with exposed rafter tails, low-profile dormers, and shallow-pitched roof of this early-twentieth-century house.

The third house on the block sits atop a low terrace far back from the sidewalk. A set of marble steps leads from the ground level to a landing, where another flight of steps leads to the front porch. The original terracotta roof is present, adding immeasurable character to the facade. I spot Art Nouveau styling in the delicate leaded and stained-glass windows, the cast flower medallions that ornament the porch railing, and the unusual roof dormer.

The house at the corner of Hillary has an inviting porch, which extends across the front of the house and around the right side. The main body of the house has a hipped roof, but a prominent and steeply pitched front gable animates the facade over the front door. The gable features a small balcony with a turned wood railing as well as Palladian-like windows.

7800 block of Pearl Street

THE BLOCK: The 7800 block of Pearl Street, on the odd-numbered or north side of the street, between Burdette Street on the east and Fern Street on the west. The block is located in Carrollton's Black Pearl neighborhood, the pie-shaped area between St. Charles Avenue on the north, Broadway on the east, and the Mississippi River on the south and west.

The streetcar links the Black Pearl to other Carrollton neighborhoods as well as to Uptown and the Central Business District (CBD). Assets include Audubon Park, just a few blocks toward downtown, and the great green expanse of the Mississippi River levee, where dogs and their owners frolic every day. Thanks to its location on high ground close to the river, the neighborhood escaped flooding in Hurricane Katrina but was dealt a devastating blow in February 2007 when a tornado ripped through the area. Each Tuesday, the Crescent City Farmers Market sets up shop in the parking lot of the former Uptown Square shopping center, drawing shoppers from throughout the city.

THE HOUSES: The seven houses on the block include a 1940s cottage, two shotgun doubles in the Neoclassical Revival style, two Craftsman-style single shotguns, a Creole cottage, and an Italianate single shotgun.

ANATOMY OF THE BLOCK: I have seen the grander houses along Broadway and St. Charles so today I explore the interior of the Black Pearl neighborhood, where I find a more varied mix of house sizes, styles, and types.

I start at the corner of Pearl and Fern and walk east, first encountering a 1940s cottage. It is wide and low and sits far back from the sidewalk, a precursor to the ranch houses built in the 1950s. Next door to it is a classic Creole cottage. Its facade, punctuated by two pairs of shuttered French doors and two windows, sits on the front property line, contrasting with its neighbor on the left. The side-gabled roof slopes steeply toward the sidewalk before changing to a more shallow pitch. The cottage almost fills the lot, leaving only enough room on each side for the narrow alley.

Coming up on the third house, I find what appears to have been a double, now converted to a single. The pale yellow house has the proportions and wide, low dormer of an early-twentieth-century Neoclassical Revival-style house. The iron fence at the sidewalk encloses a small front yard.

An Italianate single shotgun with a side wing and entry comes next. Its columns are chamfered (or beveled) with oversized spandrels forming arches between them. A turned ball and finial accents the center of each arch.

Craftsman-style shotgun singles are the fifth and sixth houses. Both houses sit back a short distance from the sidewalk and have half-wood columns atop brick or stucco pedestals emblematic of this style house. The blue one has something extra: a gable front with Tudor Revival detailing.

At the end of the block at Burdette, I find a double shotgun converted to a single in the Neoclassical Revival style. It has fluted columns, an attic dormer with multicolored glass in the sash of the attic window, and diamond-shaped panes in the sash of the front porch windows.

7500 block of Zimpel Street

THE BLOCK: The 7500 block of Zimpel Street, on the odd-numbered or north side of the street, between Cherokee Street on the east and Hillary Street on the west. A few blocks in one direction are the cafés and shops of Maple Street and a few in the other are the Tulane and Loyola campuses.

The street's name can be attributed to Charles Zimpel, a planner hired by early Carrollton developers to lay out the street grid. Though Zimpel's name is officially spelled "Zimpel," many locals, street signs, and city records spell it "Zimple."

THE HOUSES: Eight houses, including two two-story homes, five double shotguns, and one single. The predominant style is Neoclassical Revival, suggesting that the homes were built in the first decades of the twentieth century.

ANATOMY OF THE BLOCK: I pick the 7500 block for its array of colorful houses and blooming crape myrtles. I start at the corner of Hillary and move east, spending time in front of a two-story house set back from the sidewalk on a large lot. Though the second-floor porch has been enclosed, some Neoclassical Revival elements remain, like the round, tapered columns and diamond-patterned transom over the double-entry door.

A Neoclassical Revival double shotgun is next door. Instead of being set back, it is built right to the sidewalk, putting its intact details on full display. The front gable is filled with decorative shingles surrounding a three-part gable window. Tuscan columns are present, as they were next door, and so are the diamond-shaped glass panes present in the top sash of the porch windows.

The third house is painted ice blue and has a front gable and a two-story porch. One of its most distinguishing features is the row of decorative corbels in its gable, also present along the edge of the eaves.

Another Neoclassical Revival-style house appears next. This one has a hipped roof and dormer rather than a front gable. The sash in the dormer are diamond patterned and filled with stained glass, as are the transoms and the top sash of the porch windows. This house has Ionic columns instead of the simpler Tuscan style, and I see there are cloth shades rolled up between them, ready to provide shade when unfurled on a sunny day.

I pass up the next three houses—two shotguns and a cottage—and skip ahead to the corner of Cherokee Street where I find a gray house with a red door and fabulous garden. It has a low, white picket fence and an abundance of blooming crape myrtles, pale pink and white in front and along the side. A traditional copper-colored shrimp plant grows inside the fence.

1000 block of Dublin Street

THE BLOCK: The 1000 block of Dublin Street, on the even-numbered or west side of the street, between Zimpel Street on the north and Freret Street on the south. The block is in the Carrollton-Riverbend neighborhood, a triangular area bounded by Hickory Street on the north, South Carrollton Avenue on the east, and the Mississippi River on the third side.

The neighborhood maintains a small-town feel, with Oak Street serving as the community's commercial district and Carrollton Avenue as its residential boulevard. Eateries, music clubs, and shops on Oak, Carrollton, Dublin, Dante, and Hampson draw customers from all over the city. On the day I visit, plans are in full swing for the New Orleans Po-Boy Preservation Festival.

THE HOUSES: Four houses, including three two-stories from the late nineteenth or early twentieth centuries, and a one-story from the 1930s or 1940s. Two of the two-story houses are large single-family residences; the

other is a double. All are set back from the sidewalk, and a few have appealing gardens that welcome visitors.

ANATOMY OF THE BLOCK: I start at the corner of Dublin and Freret and walk north, visiting first a two-story house painted a striking shade of rose with crisp white trim and green shutters. I see porches at both levels of the house and a trellised garden on the Freret Street side. This house appears to be a single-family home now, but the four openings across the front suggest it may have been a double originally. Projections from the eaves, visible only when looking at the house from an angle because of the cypress tree, add more weight to the theory.

Next door is a two-story double

with a hipped roof, tall windows on the first floor, and milled brackets under the roof overhang on the second. I pick out other features, too, like the quoins on the trim boards on each side. Before long, I conclude that the house likely had porches across the full width of the front at both the first and second levels. If so, then the upstairs windows, now paneled at the bottom, probably originally extended from the floor to the ceiling and offered a tall opening for residents to walk through to reach the second-floor porch. A pretty little 1930s-era brick cottage is the third house on the walk. It's the only brick house on the block and the only house on the block built at grade rather than raised off the ground. Metal awnings shield the windows from sun and the front entry from rain. The awnings here are striped and add a festive flair, which is underscored by the persimmon-colored front door and pots of colorful crotons.

The fourth house is a two-story single painted a soft color with green-bronze shutters and a pumpkin-colored door. This house is embellished with millwork brackets and inviting porches across the front at both levels.

Its garden almost steals the show. Roses climb an arched trellis over the entry gate. Low yellow and deep orange flowers line the fence along the brick sidewalk and chartreuse vines line the street-side bed. In lieu of a lawn, the area behind the fence is planted with a variety of seasonal blooms, almost like a meadow. You can't appreciate it by driving by; it demands to be viewed on foot.

8300 block of Willow Street

THE BLOCK: The 8300 block of Willow Street, on the even-numbered or south side of the street, between Dante Street on the east and Cambronne Street on the west. The block is representative of New Orleans' older neighborhoods, with a mix of modest-scale houses in the middle of the block anchored by a corner store at one end and another commercial building at the other. The streetcar barn is just a block closer to Carrollton in one direction, and the shops and cafés of Oak Street are two blocks south.

THE HOUSES: Five single shotguns, a bungalow, and two Craftsman double shotguns, bracketed by commercial buildings.

ANATOMY OF THE BLOCK: I start at the corner of Dante and walk east, pausing first at the Stop & Carry Grocery. I am out early so it isn't open yet, but I can admire the exterior: a dazzling white with cheery lettering in Mardi Gras colors.

Next door is a nicely proportioned single shotgun with Arts and Crafts details like exposed rafter tails and a front door with a fan light above and sidelights. As I walk on, I realize the house is a camelback and much bigger than it looks from the sidewalk.

The next two single shotguns may well be twins, judging from the scrollwork patterns on their brackets. Each has a distinctive paint palette that helps show off the architectural details. Next on the block is a green and white bungalow, a single-family residence with an asymmetrical facade and Craftsman details. The elements are simple—rafter tails, sidelights, lattice over the gable vents—and are balanced by the clean geometry of a hedge along the sidewalk.

A very long and deep single shotgun adjacent to the bungalow still exhibits damage from Hurricane Katrina. Its neighbors are two Craftsman-style shotgun doubles, with the flared, or "battered," wood columns resting atop red brick bases as well as the exposed rafter tails exemplary of the style.

The last house on the block is an exuberant mango-colored Craftsman single with white trim and a persimmon-colored front door, accented by ice blue on the porch ceiling. This house has an unusual roofline—a cottage roof in front with gables on the side, intersected by a shotgun roof with gables on the end. The metal roof adds an extra dimension to the look.

2000 block of Burdette Street

THE BLOCK: The 2000 block of Burdette Street, on the odd-numbered or east side of the street, between Panola Street on the north and Spruce Street on the south. A neighborhood favorite, Riccobono's Panola Street Café is at the corner across the street.

THE HOUSES: A mix of early-twentieth-century houses in a variety of styles, including five doubles and a single. On the day I visit, every house on the odd-numbered side of the street had been boarded for protection from Hurricane Gustav, which has blown through over the weekend.

ANATOMY OF THE BLOCK: I stand across the street and take in the scene before examining each house more closely. It has never occurred to me that house-boarding styles may vary, until I compare them. One house has a board nailed horizontally across a window frame to protect the glass behind it. On another, a vertical piece of plywood covers a tall front window. One house has shutters, tightly secured, leaving the shutter dogs, the iron pieces that hold the shutters open, idle. On yet another house, boards are cut precisely to fit over the glass and are secured with sliding bolts.

I start at the corner of Burdette and Panola and walk south toward Spruce. The corner house looks as though it may have started life as a Craftsman double, before being converted to a single. A recent owner has added fanciful trim and strung colorful Tibetan prayer flags along the fence. As I note the tightly closed shutters, I am reminded that shutters aren't just attractive; they are highly functional in a storm.

Next door is an arresting blue Neoclassical Revival house, also a double. Here I see precisely cut boards protecting the glass in doors and windows, held in place with sliding bolts. Judging from the menacing message addressed to looters and written on one of the boards, the homeowner must remember problems that arose after Hurricane Katrina.

At the single shotgun next door, a piece of oriented strand board, or OSB, covers the long front window. The house is almost invisible behind an immense cypress tree in the front yard. Its broad base of roots and tapering form make it perfectly suited to the high winds that come with hurricanes. It has lost some foliage, though, which releases a pleasant piney scent as I walk by.

Adjacent is the house with the OSB cut into neat sections, installed to cover the front windows as well as the gable window in the attic. Next door I hear a generator running and note OSB covering the windows and glass on the doors. At the double at the end of the block, just one window is protected with wood. I can tell that this resident is well prepared for life without power when I see the two barbecue pits and a couple of folding chairs in the yard.

2300 block of Dublin Street

THE BLOCK: The 2300 block of Dublin Street, on the even-numbered or west side of the street, between South Claiborne Avenue on the north and Neron Place on the south. The block faces historic Palmer Park, where the Arts Council of New Orleans sponsors a festive arts market one Saturday each month. Conveniences include the streetcar, a bank, a drugstore, and a long-awaited grocery store, all within a two-block radius.

THE HOUSES: Six houses, including two large homes on terraced lots close to Neron Place, a single shotgun, a midcentury brick split-level, a singular house composed of two Craftsman camelbacks joined by a "bridge," and a new house under construction.

Styles are representative of those popular in New Orleans in the early twentieth century, including Mediterranean Revival, Craftsman, and Beaux Arts. Several homes are monumental in scale, but others are more modest.

ANATOMY OF THE BLOCK: I start at the corner of Neron Place and walk north toward South Claiborne Avenue. The first house is a show-stopper, though it doesn't really fit neatly into any architectural category. I note elements of the Mediterranean Revival style in its stucco exterior, red tile roof, and deep eaves. But it also features Beaux Arts elements such as banded block columns, cartouches (stucco shieldlike ornamentation), art-glass windows, and cast-flower medallions. There is an unusual barrel-roofed dormer and lushly planted garden. I would love to sit on the front porch and look out at the oaks of Palmer Park while streetcars rattle by a block away.

Next door is another house that defies easy categorization. Like the first house, it is large and occupies a terraced lot. Instead of stucco, this one is sided in wood, except for a band of stucco at the very top of the walls near the roof. Someone clever with color noticed this feature and painted the stucco band a deep dark green to contrast with the café au lait of the body. An unusual railing on the second-floor porch and ornamentation on the wood box columns both suggest the hand of a master designer or craftsman.

A diminutive single shotgun sits next door, much more intimate in scale than the two houses to its left. I appreciate the contrast in proportion and style with the two large neighbors. If this house matched them in scale, the block might seem overbuilt.

A few steps closer to Claiborne, a red brick split-level serves as a punctuation mark, a prelude to the fascinating house next door that at first looks like two separate camelback houses. But the twin houses are joined together toward the rear by a wing at the second level, creating a kind of breezeway and entry to a rear court and carriage house.

The conjoined camelbacks feature an assortment of Craftsman features, like exposed rafter tails, mitered boards at the corners, and multipaned top sashes over simpler bottoms. All are highlighted with skillful color selection and placement.

At the corner of Dublin and South Claiborne, I see a large home under construction. I think for a minute and remember the raised-basement house that used to be here before it was knocked off its foundation by the February 2007 tornado. I am pleased to see that the design of this replacement seems to take a cue from its neighbors. Aren't those exposed rafter tails at the roofline?

42 to 56 Fontainebleau Drive

THE BLOCK: A block on the south side of Fontainebleau Drive, between Adams Street on the east and Burdette Street on the west. House numbers along this stretch of Fontainebleau defy the usual pattern in New Orleans and have their own idiosyncratic logic to them, ranging from 42 to 56.

The block is located in Carrollton's Fontainebleau neighborhood, bounded roughly by Walmsley Avenue on the north, South Claiborne Avenue on the south, Broadway on the east, and South Carrollton Avenue on the west. Dairy farms could still be found here as recently as the early 1900s, when the neighborhood's major era of development occurred.

THE HOUSES: Five houses, including four in stucco with a range of Mediterranean Revival features and one in wood, which owes some of its personality to the Craftsman style. Two of the houses have a raised-basement plan, meaning the basement is at ground level and living area is above.

ANATOMY OF THE BLOCK: I stand at the corner of Adams Street, preparing to walk west toward Burdette, and admire a spectacular live oak tree twisting its branches around a Mediterranean Revival-style villa. The house exhibits all the features that make this style so picturesque—creamy stucco walls with a red tile roof, lots of variation of forms and rooflines, and exquisite features like a lovely bank of windows on the right and square tower in the middle. Even the chimney, in stucco with a red tile roof, has a style of its own. In key places, stucco ornamentation emphasizes important features like the recessed entry and the windows in the tower.

Next door on the right, the sole wood house on the block spreads out horizontally on either side of a central entry with glass front doors. The round columns at the entry provide a Colonial Revival accent. The proportions of the house, the low slope of the roof, and other features suggest this house owes most of its character to the Craftsman movement. I notice that the eaves of the side gables are deep and supported by brackets.

The third house on the block is another Mediterranean Revival-style house, but unlike the sprawling villa at the corner of Adams, this one has a vertical accent because of its raised-basement form. Steps leading from the sidewalk to the living area are tiered—a few steps, then a landing, then a few more, and so on—so that the stairs cascade rhythmically from the porch to the ground. Three rounded-top windows on the left, separated by corkscrew "Solomonic" columns, serve as the inspiration for the pair of windows on the right.

The next house is also a raised basement, but with less of a Mediterranean Revival feel. It, nonetheless, has handsome red tile steps leading up to the entry porch as well as a red tile roof and banks of casement windows.

At Burdette, I am standing again in front of a high-style Mediterranean Revival beauty. The stucco ornamentation and balustrade above the recessed entry remind me of something I might see on a Spanish Colonial church. Other intriguing features are the rounded crenellations over a bank of windows on the right and the thick, rough texturing of the home's stucco finish.

Trianon Plaza

THE BLOCK: Trianon Plaza (one block long), on the odd-numbered or east side of the street, between Walmsley Avenue on the north and Broad Place on the south, just outside the boundaries of the Fontainebleau neighborhood. The Trianon Development Corporation established the street as a residential park in 1924 and took out ads a year later touting its "Spanish-Moorish design" and modern conveniences like underground wiring and asphalt paving.

THE HOUSES: A total of twelve houses were built on Trianon Plaza (about half on each side of the street) between 1926 and 1928, most in the Spanish Revival or Spanish Eclectic style popularized by the 1915 Panama-California Exposition in San Diego. The exception is a handsome Colonial Revival house.

ANATOMY OF THE BLOCK: Although all of the houses on the street are different, all of them (except the Colonial Revival) share similar features. The Spanish Eclectic houses are generally stucco with terracotta tile roofs. All have asymmetrical massing and picturesque elements like shallow balconies, wrought iron details, arched openings, and niches.

Near the corner of Walmsley, the residents have had some fun with color. They've painted some of the roof tiles and stucco niches shades of blue, yellow, and salmon. Next door, tiered stairs lead to a vivid blue entry door. I notice the house has at least three levels, perhaps a raised basement, the entry level, and the main living level. Arched windows fill a bay that cantilevers out from the front wall of the main floor.

The adjacent house, a butterscotch hue, echoes the three-arched-window idea, but this time the bay is recessed rather than cantilevered. The finish on the stucco here is rough, almost swirled, and I see in it the hand of the artisan who worked on the house. Next door, there are just two arched-top windows so the bay is narrower with an accent on the vertical. A fancy cartouche, an applied plaster medallion, features a 3-D crown and fleur de lis. Who chose this and why? I know there has to be a story, as there is for the panel over the entry door, with its griffins and imperial lion.

You can't see the front door of the next house from the sidewalk; it's recessed inside of a portico that extends out to enclose a screened front porch. The trio of windows appear again, but this time they are capped by a wide fan window. An understated, engaged tower on the second floor forecasts what I will see at the end of the block.

Now I stand in front of a Colonial Revival house with a recessed entry and mitered corners. It bears no stylistic relationship with the other houses on the block, but I recognize it as a member of the same generation. The era in which "revival" styles (be they Spanish or American Colonial) were the rage.

Now I take a close look at the sparkling white house I see whenever I make the turn from Broadway onto Broad Place toward St. Rita's Church. There's the tower again, but it's rounded here and almost disengaged from the building. The red tile roof, the stucco walls, the wrought iron finial on the tower, the arched windows recessed in a niche in the wall are all elements of other houses on the block that appear again here. Yet this house is very different in its layout and footprint. One wing is perpendicular to Trianon Plaza, the other parallel, and the round tower appears at the intersection of the two.

8200 block of Apricot Street

THE BLOCK: The 8200 block of Apricot Street, on the even-numbered or south side of the street, between Dublin Street on the east and Dante Street on the west, in the Northwest Carrollton neighborhood. A few blocks away on Carrollton is the chateauesque Notre Dame Seminary. The College Inn restaurant has been a fixture in the neighborhood for decades on Carrollton, and businesses have opened up along Earhart, including a recently relocated Rock 'n' Bowl. At the corner of Dante and Apricot stands Incarnate Word Church, a masterpiece of Spanish Colonial Revival architecture.

THE HOUSES: A mix of types and styles, including three spectacular Craftsman bungalows, two two-story duplexes, and a Neoclassical Revival double shotgun. The duplexes and shotgun, though unrenovated, all have terrific potential. A vacant lot in the middle of the block marks the spot where the February 2007 tornado ripped through, destroying a raised-basement house.

ANATOMY OF THE BLOCK: I start at the corner of Dublin and walk west toward Dante. The first house is a gray-shingled bungalow with white trim, red sash, and arresting Craftsman details that beg for a closer look. Like the most interesting of Craftsman houses, this one has multiple rooflines; gable detailing, which serves as attic ventilation; exposed rafter tails; clustered columns atop stone pedestals; and an entry composed of multipaned doors with sidelights. The floor plan and facade are asymmetrical in true bungalow style with a front-gabled entry on the right of the house and the end-gabled wing on the left.

The foundation stands out, because it is sheathed in stucco embedded with hefty chunks of rock and boulders, a high-style Craftsman feature. In California, where the treatment originated, the rocks and boulders expressed the preference for using native materials. Though such geological specimens aren't a natural part of our river delta environment, plenty of smooth boulders made their way to our port city as ballast on ships. Maybe some of those I see were ballast stones.

Next door, a vivid red bungalow nestles behind a white picket fence and a profusion of blooms and color. Wonderful details include shingles, boulders in the chimney, bays, and banks of windows. Unlike shotgun houses, which usually don't have architectural features on their sides, Craftsman bungalows like this one are often as interesting from the side as they are from the front.

The third house, a buttery yellow, departs slightly from the pattern established by the first two. It is covered in stucco rather than wood shingles, and the columns that support the porch overhang are stucco instead of wood. Like the first two houses, though, it has an asymmetrical facade and floor plan. The low, wide dormer in the side wing is a hallmark of the style, as are the multipaned windows.

I pass a lot left vacant by the 2007 tornado and study two up-down duplexes and a Neoclassical Revival double shotgun at the end of the block. They need to be renovated to bring out all of their appealing features, but even in their current condition, I note the front porches, the arched tops over the doors on the duplexes, and the lovely diamond-patterned stained glass on the shotgun.

8900 block of Edinburgh Street

THE BLOCK: The 8900 block of Edinburgh Street, on the odd-numbered or north side of the street, between General Ogden on the east and Hollygrove on the west. The block is located in Carrollton's Hollygrove neighborhood, familiar to nonresidents as the home of the Carrollton Boosters sports facility and, more recently, the Hollygrove Market and Farm on the former Guillot's Nursery site.

Hollygrove didn't develop until advances in drainage made the area habitable in the early decades of the twentieth century. By the 1960s, when New Orleans' population was at its peak, almost all of Hollygrove was built up. Dwayne Michael "Lil Wayne" Carter, Jr., may be the Hollygrove-bred artist best known today, but rhythm and blues legend Johnny Adams put Hollygrove on the map musically long before Lil Wayne's rise to stardom.

THE HOUSES: A group of nine houses, all one story and dating from about the 1930s to 1950s.

ANATOMY OF THE BLOCK: I start at the corner of Edinburgh and Hollygrove and walk east, pausing in front of the first house on the block, the only one that hasn't been rehabilitated since Hurricane Katrina. It's probably just a matter of time before it is revived, judging from the abundant renovation activity and new construction I spot in the area. The next house is mango-colored, faced in stucco, and accented with glossy black cast iron columns and railing. A couple of low steps lead to an entry porch. Like many houses on either side of the block, this one has a place to sit on the porch—a metal loveseat.

The neighboring brick house has

similar proportions, but a shallow wing extends forward from the main body of the house, its roof turning a gable end toward the street. The owner has built a brick-columned carport on half of the front yard. A few steps farther and I am in front of a brick house with a hipped roof and a terrazzo-style path leading from the sidewalk to the front steps. The forward wing of the house is sheathed in wood (or lookalike) siding and serves as a garage instead of living space.

The pink brick house that follows is built at grade, level with the parking area in front. In the shade created by a gable-ended roof extension, folding chairs provide a place to sit and watch the street. The red brick house next door occupies the largest lot on the block, double the size of the others from the looks of it. A grassy lawn stretches from the house to the sidewalk, and an iron fence with brick pillars encircles the home.

The pale yellow stucco house next door has a gabled-fronted

garage and cast-iron-railed entry porch paved in stone. Two chairs have been installed for afternoon porch sitting.

The last house on the block breaks the mold as far as the architecture of the rest of the block goes. Parisian mint green with forest green trim, this storybook-style double cottage has a steeply pitched roof over the entry and rounded-top entry doors. The gable window over the doors repeats the rounded-top detail. The cottage sits almost a foot higher off the ground than its neighbors, so the chairs on its porch offer an elevated view.

9200 block of Palm Street

THE BLOCK: The 9200 block of Palm Street, on the odd-numbered or north side of the street, between Mistletoe Street on the east and Cherry Street on the west. The block is in the Palm-Air subdivision, called North Hollygrove by some and Dixon by others, just off Airline Highway.

Palm-Air was developed in the late 1930s by Wallace C. Walker, whose firm also developed Cortez Homes (between Xavier University and South Jefferson Davis Parkway) and Park Place (bounded by Florida and Navarre, Marconi and Marshall Foch) in New Orleans. In Mississippi, the company developed a portion of Pass Christian. Another of Walker's legacies was the mid-twentieth-century widening of Tulane Avenue to create the "Miracle Mile."

THE HOUSES: There are six houses on the block, each separated from the sidewalk by a generous front lawn and each having its own driveway and sometimes garage. Some are split-levels and one has a garage integral to the house. Most are renovated and occupied, but some are still awaiting repair from flooding in Hurricane Katrina.

ANATOMY OF THE BLOCK: I begin at the corner of Cherry and walk east, first studying the corner house. It is a split-level consisting of a cottage on the left and two-story wing on the right. The ground floor of the two-story portion serves as a garage. The roof over the cottage portion has a double pitch and a well-proportioned and detailed dormer. The roof extends out past the front wall of the house, creating a shaded porch. The two-story wing has a hipped roof. As I walk past, I notice that the garage wing extends far backward and the house is much larger than it appears from the front.

A few steps more and I am in front of a cottage with a tile roof. The primary form of the house is somewhat like a Cape Cod cottage with a side gable, but there is also a front-gabled portion in the center of the front that extends forward. The walkway follows a sinuous route from the sidewalk to the front steps, a "storybook" element.

The third house follows much the same form as the first house, with some differences. There is no porch across the front but an emphasized entry instead. And though there was once a garage on the first floor of the two-story wing (I can see the drive strips), the former garage space has been converted to living space. I also notice an extension off the left side, which I bet used to be a screened-in porch before being enclosed as living space.

Next comes another version of the cross-gabled house, but this time with a screened-in front porch under the front gable. A few other details are different (the gable window, for example), but overall, I think I am starting to see how the developer took a few house forms and mixed and matched the porches, entries, side wings, and roof details to create a varied streetscape.

The next two houses are sheathed in brick, rather than in wood siding like the first four. At first, I consider whether they are more recent additions to the block or originals that have been altered. I conclude that they are the latter; the proportions, the roof slopes, and a few other details tip the balance and convince me.

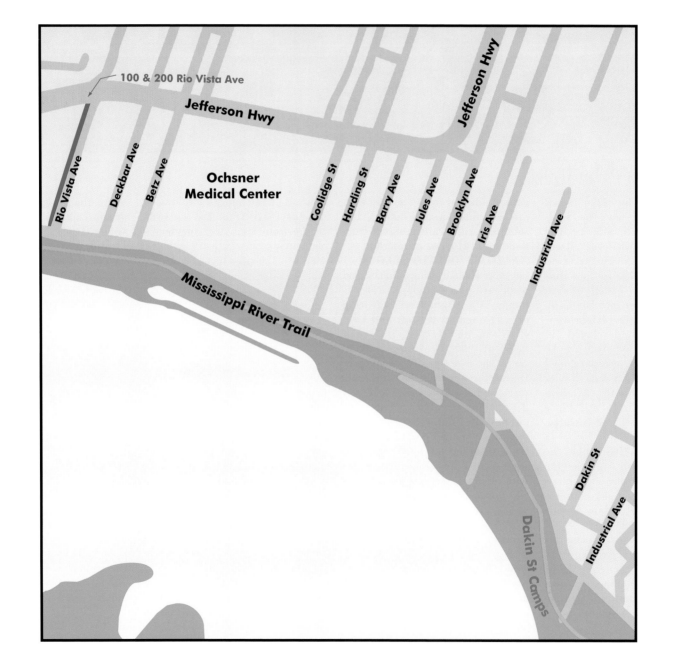

Old Jefferson

The history of Jefferson Parish is inextricably intertwined with that of Orleans Parish. In fact, many neighborhoods in New Orleans were once part of Jefferson Parish but were annexed gradually to Orleans over the decades.

Just as the natural levees of the Mississippi River provided attractive high ground for Orleans Parish settlements, they also attracted development in Jefferson. Today, there are many riverside communities in Jefferson to explore on both the Eastbank and the Westbank, but the two featured here offer a bit of insight into the area's interesting history and neighborhoods.

Dakin Street Campsites

THE BLOCK: Campsites Nos. 1 through 12 on the river batture in Jefferson Parish, immediately adjacent to the Jefferson-Orleans Parish line, located between the intersections of Dakin Street and Monticello Avenue with River Road and the levee. Nearby is Southport Hall, once a storied gambling establishment but now a music and party venue.

Although some sources define "batture" as the strip of land between the river and the levee, other sources indicate it is the portion of the Mississippi River bed exposed to air when river levels are low. The changing character of the land hasn't kept people from establishing residences—referred to by Jefferson Parish as "camps"—atop pilings over the water and at its edge. A colony of more than one hundred batture dwellings once stretched for two miles upriver of Audubon Park and into Jefferson Parish, according to University of New Orleans professor Michael Mizell-Nelson, but decades of levee repair and expansion projects beginning in the mid-1950s caused most batture dwellers to move.

THE HOUSES: An assortment of twelve structures atop pilings, some resembling the informal camps most commonly associated with waterside dwellings, others looking more like urban residences. When trees on the batture are bare, rooftops of the dwellings are visible from River Road.

ANATOMY OF THE BLOCK: I start at the west end of the encampment close to where Monticello Avenue meets the levee and walk east. I pass the first camp, a pink building with a metal roof and a camper top at its side. A few steps farther and I am looking at a fishing camp straight out of central casting. It has a wide porch all around, driftwood inserted between pilings, and buoys strung from the porch ceiling. There are even faded Barq's Root Beer signs hanging on the outside walls.

A boardwalk leads to the third dwelling, a blue camp with a faded red side wing. The fourth house camp appears to have grown by accretion, with low-pitched roofs covering each successive side addition, until the house looks as if it is wearing saddlebags.

The fifth house deserves to be called the gingerbread house, for it is an idiosyncratic amalgam of fanciful architectural elements like milled brackets, stained-glass windows, sawn balusters, and French doors, topped with a corrugated metal roof. I see roosters and hens taking dirt baths in the front yard, giving a whole new meaning to the term "free range."

A thicket of rosemary and raised bed of fennel leads the way to the sixth camp, a metal-roofed cottage with abundant windows for the spectacular views. After I pass it, I am looking at an über-contemporary house, a cheery mix of colors, forms, and materials. For all of its nontraditional elements, it seems almost tame compared to its whacky neighbors.

The adjacent wide, yellow cottage features a front porch and stained-glass windows in its dormer. Next to it, a house renovation nears completion. The portion facing the levee is a single story, but it has a two-story wing on the river side that angles out toward the water to capture the views. The tenth camp, a green and white house, has a pond with statuary and deck pierced by a large sycamore tree.

When I reach the last two camps, I feel as if I have made a major architectural discovery. Surely, these free-form assemblages of roof slopes and siding materials have inspired—if only subliminally—the design of many of the contemporary houses being built in New Orleans today.

100 and 200 blocks of Rio Vista Avenue

THE BLOCK: The 100 and 200 blocks of Rio Vista Avenue in Old Jefferson, on the even-numbered or west side of the street, between Jefferson Highway on the north and River Road on the south. The block is situated in a subdivision by the same name, developed in the 1930s and early 1940s by John L. Lauricella and Associates. The developer named the area Rio Vista for "River View," owing to its proximity to the Mississippi River.

In original promotional materials for the project, the developer cited the quality of materials and workmanship used in constructing each house. Amenities included private bedrooms (in contrast with the walk-through bedrooms of older shotgun houses), built-in medicine cabinets and linen closets, abundant electrical outlets, cypress exterior doors and weatherboards, and plaster walls. Thirty-two different house plans were offered. Masonry columns bearing the Rio Vista name mark the entrance on Jefferson Highway.

THE HOUSES: A collection of petite cottages set back and separated from the sidewalk by expanses of closely cropped grass, flanked by driveways and often having garages. Though all were a modest size when built (1,000 to 1,500 square feet), many have been added onto over the years to accommodate larger families.

ANATOMY OF THE BLOCK: I learn while visiting Rio Vista that several television commercials have been shot here, and I can see why. Taken together as a whole, the cottages, green lawns, and mature trees look like a portrait of idyllic American life. Though each house has its own distinguishing characteristics—a side porch on one, a front porch on another, for example—viewed together from the sidewalk the houses present a unified look, owing to similar size and massing.

I start at River Road and walk north toward Jefferson Highway, scouting out architectural elements as I go. Some of the houses have details that were popular on Cotswold Cottage houses in the same era: a steeply pitched, asymmetrical gable that turns up on one side, plus an arched-top front door and door casing. The style was sometimes called Storybook style. Although the Rio Vista houses are built in wood and not stone like the Cotswold Cottages, the reference is unmistakable.

Another Storybook element I notice are the curving pathways leading from the sidewalk to the entries of some of the houses, as well as the arched-top roof vents placed prominently in some forward-facing gables. I see many front doors with a rustic charm, including vertical boards assembled so that the seams are readily visible and prominent metal strap hinges. On other houses, circular windows are cut out of the doors and filled with glass in a diamond or crisscross pattern.

Some of the houses shun the fanciful for the sober. Many of them are clean, no-nonsense interpretations of the Colonial Revival style, often featuring dormers. All are enhanced by porches, whether on the front, in the center, or to one side.

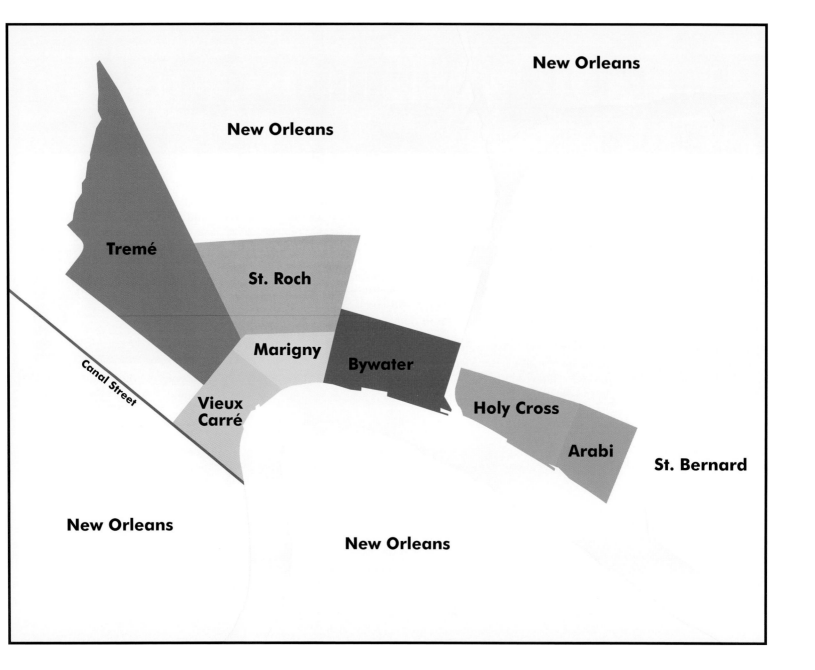

Section II
Downriver of Canal Street

Canal Street serves as the great divide in New Orleans, the line between downtown and Uptown, the Creole city and the Anglo city, with a neutral ground, known as a median in other places, running right down the middle of the wide boulevard. And though these divisions date back to 1803 and the sale of the French-owned Louisiana Territory to the United States, the cultural differences between the Creoles and the Anglos continue to influence the character of their respective neighborhoods even today.

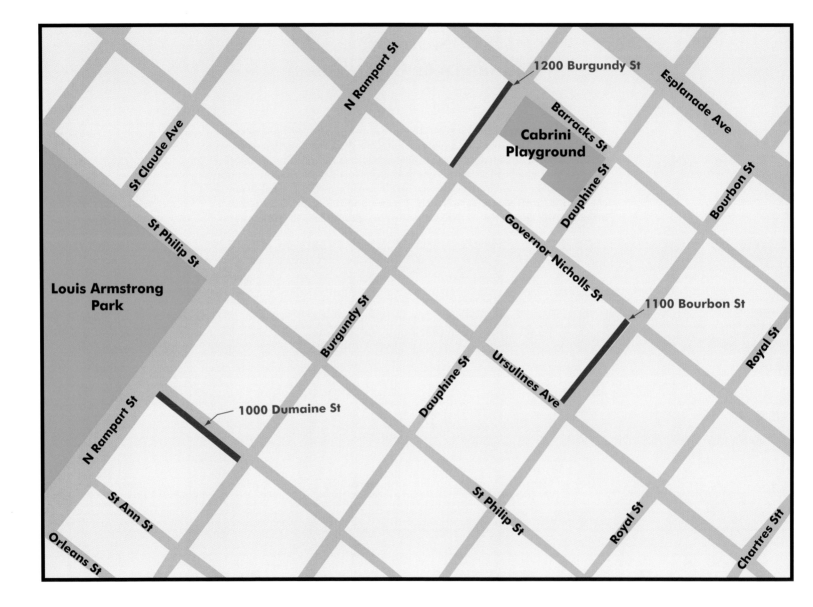

Vieux Carré

The storied Vieux Carré or Old Square is at the heart of New Orleans' Creole neighborhoods and is the location of La Nouvelle Orleans, founded in 1718. The Vieux Carré is a national landmark and was added to the National Register in the 1960s, several decades after the Vieux Carré Commission was established by an act of the Louisiana legislature in 1936. Once enclosed by fortifications, the Vieux Carré is bounded by North Rampart Street on the north, the Mississippi River on the south, Esplanade Avenue on the east, and Canal Street on the west.

By about 1721, French engineers under the direction of Adrien de Pauger had laid out a grid of streets for the young city. The plan featured an open parade ground, now Jackson Square, with a church facing it. Much of the area's French and Spanish colonial architecture (except for the Ursulines Convent) was lost in devastating fires of 1788 and 1794. Nonetheless, Creole cottages and townhouses from the early 1800s mix with later types and styles to establish the Quarter's European flavor.

With dining, music, and other nightlife activities concentrated closer to Canal Street, the area of the Quarter closest to Esplanade retains a strong residential character. For all the hoopla over its tourist attractions, the French Quarter is first and foremost a neighborhood, continuously occupied for more than two hundred years.

Several nonprofit organizations work to maintain the quality of residential life in the Vieux Carré, and the Vieux Carré Commission, a municipal agency, strives to maintain the quality and appropriateness of changes to its priceless inventory of historic structures.

1100 block of Bourbon Street

THE BLOCK: The 1100 block of Bourbon Street, on the odd-numbered or north side of the street, between Governor Nicholls Street and Ursulines Avenue. Anchoring the Ursulines end of the block is the Quarter Launderette and Dry Cleaners, an establishment offering essential services to nearby residents. Across the street, the Quarter Master deli is patronized almost exclusively by locals rather than the visitors who jam the more well-trodden parts of the Vieux Carré.

THE HOUSES: A vibrantly colored collection of buildings reflecting more than 120 years of the city's history, including a duo of Creole cottages, several shotgun houses, and a trio of fine masonry townhouses.

ANATOMY OF THE BLOCK: The day I visit, the sky is a stunning shade of blue and is a perfect foil for the riot of colors I find on the block: rich salmon, buttery yellow, turquoise, rose, purple, gray green. It's true that the Vieux Carré is the only local historic district in which color is regulated, but who cares when there is clearly so much to choose from?

I start at the corner of Bourbon and Ursulines at the Quarter Launderette and walk east. The business is housed in a modified Creole cottage converted into a commercial space. It has an intriguing roof, which is hipped on three sides, and it sits right up on the sidewalk, like most of the other buildings on the block. No doubt the scored stucco on its walls covers brick, maybe even the brick-between-post construction that was prevalent in the early years. Two sets of French doors open to an interior space.

A pristine Italianate double shotgun follows. The combination of the yellow body color, blue shutters, dark red window sash, and white trim brings out all of its architectural details: the milled brackets, the arched-top windows, the cornices, and even the soffit vents.

The third house is shielded from the street by a tall brick wall, but I catch a glimpse of Eastlake elements above the bougainvillea. I pick out the top of a turned column, sunburst brackets, and a frieze with piercework panels.

A few steps farther, I am standing in front of a Creole cottage with tall, narrow dormers. It is painted two shades of aqua, but I note that the foundation vents along the sidewalk are painted terracotta, a nice contrast. Even though the fleur-de-lis type millwork along the roof edge is not original, it's a flourish that ties the house thematically to several of its neighbors.

To be honest, I have trouble making heads or tails of the fifth house. Its steep front gable suggests Gothic Revival, but its door and window tops are segmentally arched, an Italianate feature. The roofline of the main part of the house suggests a cottage of some kind. I accept it as a happy anomaly and move on to an orchid-colored masonry townhouse with a balcony on the second floor. It has French doors shaded by deep purple shutters and a chaste row of masonry dentils across the top. Someone has taken great care to choose flowering plants that coordinate with the color scheme.

It's getting chilly, and I skimp a bit on the buildings at the end of the block, three more townhouses and a tiny one-story shotgun, wedged in between its two tall neighbors. I linger just long enough to note the frilly cast iron ornamentation on two of the townhouses.

1200 block of Burgundy Street

THE BLOCK: The 1200 block of Burgundy Street, on the odd-numbered or north side of the street, located between Barracks Street on the east and Governor Nicholls Street on the west. With restaurants and nightclubs concentrated closer to Canal Street, the 1200 block of Burgundy is residential, except for the fabled Cosimo's Bar at one end and what's known as the "dog park" (more formally Cabrini Park) across the street.

THE HOUSES: Five houses, including four Creole cottages punctuated by a stately two-story townhouse. The cottage at the corner of Governor Nicholls has a two-story structure at the rear, which is either a service wing or a sixth structure.

ANATOMY OF THE BLOCK: I start at the corner of Burgundy Street and Governor Nicholls, where Cosimo's stands, and walk east toward Barracks. In all my years of late-night visits to the place, I never noticed until now

that the legendary bar is housed in a large Creole cottage. I spot some details, such as the steeply pitched, side-gabled roof that makes room for living space upstairs, and note the French doors leading to a balcony over the sidewalk. The iron railing is cast rather than wrought (created from a mold rather than heated and bent into shape). A courtyard separates the cottage structure from the tall, narrow structure at the rear, which is no doubt a service wing transformed into living space.

Next door, I see another version of a Creole cottage. This one is sided in wood, rather than stucco like Cosimo's, and I see it has solid batten shutters. The slate roof on this one has an abat-vent, a metal projection that extends

from the face of the building out over the sidewalk to provide a little shade and direct rain from the roof outward and away from the building.

The third building is a tall and handsome townhouse with an entry door on the left side. I admire the stately pilasters flanking the recessed entry, the marble steps, and the candy-apple red front door. Dentils over the front entry and bricks on the parapet suggest the brick townhouse was constructed when the Greek Revival style was in vogue. To the right of the main house, a garden wall holds iron entry gates.

On the right of the townhouse is yet another Creole cottage, also wearing an abat-vent. This cottage, though, has four equal-sized openings, two doors and two full-length windows, rather than two long and two short. The shutters here are louvered on top and paneled on the bottom.

I reach the last house on the block and ask myself a dozen questions. Why are there dormers on this Creole cottage but not on the others on the block? And aren't the dormers especially tall and narrow? Is this a double or a single? I turn the questions over in my mind as I head back to Cosimo's for refreshment.

1000 block of Dumaine Street

THE BLOCK: The 1000 block of Dumaine Street, on the even-numbered or west side of the street, between North Rampart Street on the north and Burgundy Street on the south. Situated at the northern edge of the French Quarter, this block features residential buildings plus the commercial building that housed Peristyle Restaurant and, before that, Marti's. Looking toward Rampart, I see Armstrong Park.

THE HOUSES: Two Creole cottages and two townhouses plus a building that has been altered and added onto so that its original identity is unclear.

ANATOMY OF THE BLOCK: The former home of writer Tennessee Williams draws me to the block and demands my attention first. Williams owned and lived in the townhouse close to the Burgundy end of the block from 1962 until his death in 1983. There are other structures in the city with ties to the author, but this was his last residence.

The Williams home is an American-townhouse type, with two and a half stories, three openings across the front, and a front door on the right leading to a sidehall and stairs. A gallery stretches across the full width of the building on the second floor, over the sidewalk, and is supported by cast iron columns. Cast iron panels in a grapevine pattern serve as the gallery railing. A tall dormer on the roof is barely visible because of where I am standing.

Two Creole cottages follow as I walk toward North Rampart Street, and at first, I think how very different they are. The first is sheathed in stucco and has four sets of French doors and batten shutters across the front. I notice stucco bands, very subtle, across the top of and down the sides of the facade, an early decorative feature. The house has two dormers with classical details, including pilasters and a fancy design on the windowpanes.

The neighboring house is a two-bay Creole cottage, which is literally half the size of its neighbor. Stucco has been removed, exposing the brick, and there are just two sets of French doors instead of four. The shutters are different from those on the house adjacent; here they are louvered with paneled bottoms rather than solid batten shutters. Considering these differences, I am surprised to see that they share a distinctive element—the millwork detailing on the dormer. Maybe they aren't so different after all.

A bit closer to North Rampart Street is a Creole townhouse. Like Williams' American townhouse, it too has three openings across the front. Instead of a door and two windows, one of the openings is a wide archway opening to a passage that runs from the sidewalk in the front to the courtyard in the rear. This is the porte-cochere that served in the olden days as storage for the carriage when not in use.

I see another difference between this townhouse and Williams'. This one has a balcony rather than a gallery at the second level, cantilevered out from the building and extending only partially across the sidewalk. I look at the roof and realize I am seeing the same dormer details as I saw on the two Creole cottages. Could these three buildings—the two Creole cottages and the Creole townhouse—have been built at the same time?

The four fine buildings are followed by a curiosity, a building that may have started out as a two-story double shotgun before experiencing a radical transformation. Rather than continue the description, I'll stick with the term "curiosity" and leave it at that.

Tremé

Tremé is one of three neighborhoods that compose the Esplanade Ridge Historic District stretching from Bayou St. John on the north to North Rampart Street on the south and from St. Bernard Avenue on the east to Orleans Avenue on the west.

The Tremé portion of Esplanade Ridge is divided in two by the elevated I-10 overpass that replaced the avenue's oaks and shopping district in the late 1950s. The portion of Tremé closest to the French Quarter is bounded roughly by North Claiborne, North Rampart, St. Bernard, and Orleans and centered on St. Augustine Church. The portion closer to Bayou St. John is bounded by North Broad, North Claiborne, Esplanade, and Orleans and has St. Peter Claver Church as its spiritual core.

The area takes it name from Claude Tremé, who came to New Orleans from France in about 1785 and purchased much of the former Morand Plantation on Bayou Road, the portage that followed a natural ridge from Bayou St. John to the Vieux Carré. After the plantation's subdivision in the late eighteenth and early nineteenth centuries, the faubourg, or suburb, was settled by Creoles, including free people of color. Today, it nurtures many indigenous New Orleans cultural traditions, such as Mardi Gras Indian tribes, Skull and Bones gangs, second-lines, and brass bands.

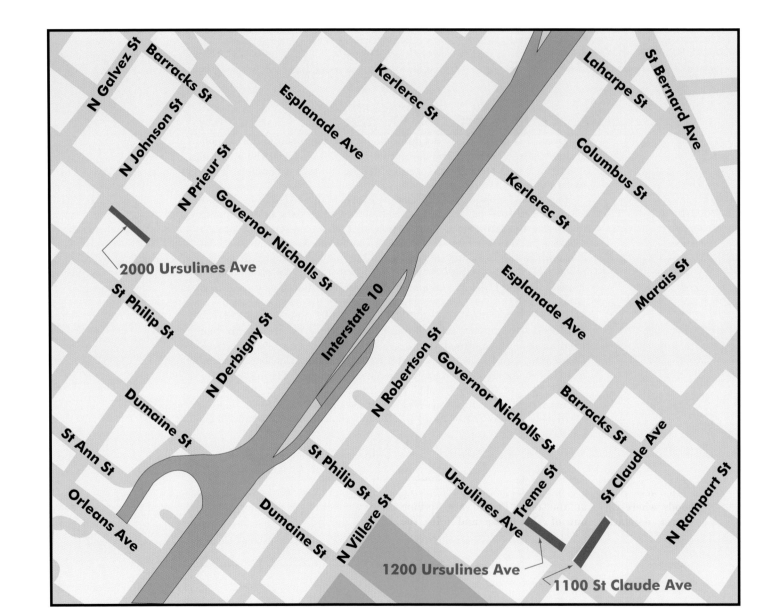

1100 block of St. Claude Avenue

THE BLOCK: The 1100 block of St. Claude Avenue on the even-numbered or south side of the street, between Governor Nicholls Street (formerly Bayou Road) on the east and Ursulines Avenue on the west. The block is home to the Backstreet Cultural Museum and close to St. Augustine Catholic Church; the New Orleans African American Museum of Art, Culture, and History; and Lil Dizzy's Café on Esplanade Avenue.

THE HOUSES: Six houses, including two double shotguns close to Governor Nicholls, two 1930s cottages (including the museum) in the middle of the block, and two masonry Creole cottages near Ursulines.

ANATOMY OF THE BLOCK: Tremé is one of the few New Orleans neighborhoods where the activity on the street regularly upstages the historic architecture, no matter how fabulous it is. I visit the block on a Carnival day, lured there by the sound of drums and chanting, and soon get a glimpse of feathers and glittering beadwork. Yes, the Mardi Gras Indians are in the street, and I stop to watch.

At the Governor Nicholls end of the block, two green double shotguns offer stoops for sitting and watching the activity. I see chairs lined up against the houses, filled with weary fans of all ages. The houses themselves appear identical—doors on the outside, windows in the center, cast-iron soffit vents, cornices above the windows, hipped roofs, and milled brackets. There is plenty of opportunity here for highlighting features like the bands of the drop-lap siding and details in the brackets. All it would take is a more adventurous paint job!

To the right of the two doubles is a shotgun single with a side wing at the rear. People are spilling out of the house and onto the front porch, eager to be part of the happenings. Exposed rafter tails in the side eaves impart a mild Craftsman flavor to the little house.

The fourth building is a Neoclassical Revival bungalow, formerly used as the Blandin Funeral Home and now as the Backstreet Cultural Museum. It is the epicenter of activity today, but while celebrants are going in and out, I step back and admire its Corinthian columns. No doubt the brick applied to the exterior was a later treatment, but the double-hipped roof and wing that projects forward on the right appear to be classic bungalow forms.

Adjacent to the museum are two masonry Creole cottages with quite a few similar features, including a common wall between them. Each has a rough stucco base at the sidewalk that transitions to smooth a couple of feet higher, and each has batten shutters over four openings. The cottage on the right, however, displays zigzag brickwork at the top of the facade, directly under the eave. I wonder if this feature is hiding on the cottage to the left, obscured by the wood soffit that has been installed.

1200 block of Ursulines Avenue

THE BLOCK: The 1200 block of Ursulines Avenue, on the odd-numbered or east side of the street, between Tremé Street on the north and St. Claude Avenue on the south. The block is located close to Tremé landmarks including St. Augustine Church.

THE HOUSES: Eight dwellings in an array of forms, styles, and especially color. There's just one two-story house on the block, and it is accompanied by seven shotgun houses—three sidehalls and four doubles. Styles range from Greek Revival to Craftsman, with Eastlake in between.

ANATOMY OF THE BLOCK: I start at the corner of Tremé and walk south, stopping to admire a lemon-yellow two-story building with a second-floor balcony. The home has a Craftsman flare thanks to deep eaves, front-facing gable, and angle brackets. Looking closely, I think I can see exposed rafter tails partially hidden by rain gutters.

A brightly painted Italianate sidehall shotgun appears next door as I continue the walk. The owner has highlighted some of its features with an eye-popping color scheme: red on the turned balusters, shutters, and sunburst pattern in the gable against a mint green body. Even the corbels under the cornices over the arched-top windows are emphasized with red.

I walk on to study a Greek Revival sidehall painted light green with pale purple shutters. It has milled brackets and three full-length openings like its neighbor but has a hipped roof (instead of gable fronted), square-top windows and shutters (not arched), and paneled bases on the louvered shutters. I notice that the cornices over the windows and door create a subtle hierarchy, for the one over the entry is taller and more detailed than over the windows, expressing its greater importance. Pilasters flank the entry and serve to underscore its stature.

The Italianate sidehall that follows is painted dusty blue, but white is used to accent the shutters, decorative millwork atop the windows, quoins on the edge boards, and trim around the gable window. Unlike its neighbors, this house is set back from the sidewalk far enough to accommodate parallel rows of evergreen hedges and an elegant black iron fence.

A quartet of fanciful Eastlake double shotguns completes the block and expands its color palette. Eastlake houses lend themselves perfectly to multicolored paint schemes because of their variety of intricate millwork features, and these take full advantage of color to enhance their natural beauty. Their form is especially interesting because their entries aren't recessed; they project forward from the front wall.

On the first of the four houses, shades of rose and green call attention to elements like the turned columns, spindles in the open frieze between columns, and sunburst pattern in the multiple gables, one over each entry and another at the peak of the roofline. The narrower bands of the drop-lap siding appear to have been painted slightly darker than the wider bands, establishing a horizontal pattern.

On the second house, sage green contrasts with the two-tone peach body of the house, drawing the eye to the cornices above the openings, shutters, and sash surrounding the stained-glass gable window. Next door, an unexpected mustard color makes the front door a focal point and stands out against the mostly dark blue body and rose-colored shutters.

The fourth house in the collection is painted a deep gold color. Its paint scheme is tame compared to that of its comrades, with a palette limited to the body color, white for the trim, dark green for the shutters, and terracotta for the front door. All the same, the colors work together well and enhance the appeal of the house.

2000 block of Ursulines Avenue

THE BLOCK: The 2000 block of Ursulines Avenue, on the odd-numbered or east side of the street, between North Johnson Street on the north and North Prieur Street on the south.

The land in this area of Tremé was once owned by Micaela de Pontalba and was known as the Pontalba Division, according to the Friends of the Cabildo's book on Faubourg Tremé. Today, however, it is better known as St. Peter Claver for the nearby church, which serves as the spiritual core of the community.

THE HOUSES: Seven houses in an assortment of types and styles, including two center-hall houses, an eccentric Tudor Revival house, a 1940s duplex, a skinny two-story house with galleries, and a couple of shotguns (one of them with lavish details).

ANATOMY OF THE BLOCK: I start at the corner of Ursulines and North Johnson and stand in front of an elegant center-hall house, admiring its handsome proportions and refined entry details. The house's facade sits at the front property line so there is no room for a porch. The entry door sits deep within a recess marked at the sidewalk with pilasters and Greek Revival-style dentils. Panels line the walls of the recess and very narrow sidelights flank the door itself. Above the door, a transom holds elliptically shaped glass and is separated from the top of the sidelights by hand-carved corbels. Narrow dormers add an element of verticality to the otherwise horizontal composition.

A nicely maintained two-story duplex is adjacent to the center-hall. Its Craftsman features date it to sometime between the 1920s and 1940s.

The third house is an original, without twins anywhere in the city that I know of. Judging from the Tudor Revival elements in the gable (the applied wood details with stucco in between), I am willing to hazard a guess that the house dates from the first few decades of the twentieth century, when revival styles were popular. But its exuberant roof line—swooping down on each side before turning up again—is in a league of its own. Am I the only one who thinks it looks like a Dutchman's hat?

Closer to North Prieur stands a narrow two-story house with porches across the front on both the first and second floors. Some details, such as the walk-through window next to the entry door, suggest a late-nineteenth-century house, but others, like the rounded columns atop a masonry base, suggest something later.

The fifth house is a raised center-hall with a central dormer. The entry is less elaborate than the one on the corner house but it is recessed, too, owing to the fact that it sits at the sidewalk with no room for a porch.

The pink house next door to it surely started out as a single shotgun or perhaps a sidehall with a Greek Revival or Italianate entablature and parapet. Over time, though, it gained several two-story additions toward the rear as well as Eastlake-style columns and an open frieze on the front. The "updates" make it a textbook example of how changing fashion can alter the appearance of a building.

A sidehall shotgun stands next to the pink house at the corner of North Prieur. It appears to have gained a two-story wing sometime after it was built, plus a garage addition on its left side. When the house was constructed, cars weren't a factor in design, so the owner simply added on.

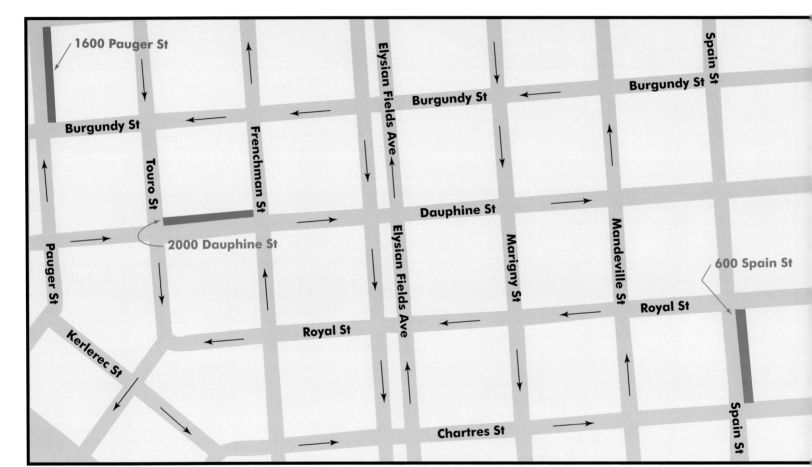

Faubourg Marigny

Faubourg Marigny is one of New Orleans' oldest faubourgs, or suburbs, situated just across Esplanade from the French Quarter. Its origins date to about 1805, when landowner Bernard Xavier Phillippe de Marigny de Mandeville subdivided his plantation into lots according to a plan devised by Nicholas de Finiels and laid out by Barthelemy Lafon. By then, thousands of refugees from slave revolts in Haiti had inundated the city of New Orleans, and Marigny had attracted many of these French-speaking expatriates to his neighborhood by offering to sell them property with no down payment.

Named to the National Register of Historic Places in 1974, Faubourg Marigny is bounded roughly by North Rampart Street/St. Claude Avenue on the north, the Mississippi River on the south, Press Street on the east, and Esplanade Avenue on the west. Locals distinguish between two areas of the neighborhood: Marigny Triangle west of Elysian Fields Avenue and Marigny Rectangle east of it.

Elysian Fields Avenue was originally the site of a canal that served Marigny Plantation's sawmill, according to research by the Faubourg Marigny Improvement Association. The canal was filled in and sold to the Pontchartrain Railroad in 1830.

Today, Washington Square still provides a leafy retreat from the tightly packed streets, while the clubs and cafés of Frenchmen Street draw music and food fans from all over. In 2009, Marigny's walkable streets, fascinating architecture, and collection of sidewalk businesses attracted the attention of the American Planning Association and earned the neighborhood a spot on the group's annual list of 10 Great Neighborhoods.

1600 block of Pauger Street

THE BLOCK: The 1600 block of Pauger Street, on the odd-numbered or east side of the street, between North Rampart Street on the north and Burgundy Street on the south. The block is situated in the Marigny Triangle area, hidden in a maze of streets that bend at odd angles and are confusing to walkers as well as drivers.

THE HOUSES: Seven houses including a centerpiece of four Creole cottages, bracketed at one end by a two-story corner storehouse and a shotgun double and on the other end by a walled house and courtyard.

ANATOMY OF THE BLOCK: Although the block displays a variety of house types, its components share several distinctive characteristics that define the personality of the block. First and foremost, the block is dancing with vivid color. Second, all of the houses come right up to the sidewalk, having no front yards whatsoever. Due to the lack of space between the buildings and the sidewalk, the houses

have stoops instead of porches. Third, all have gated alleys with gates built at the same height and painted colors that coordinate with those of the houses.

I start at the North Rampart end of the block and walk south, starting with the two-story corner storehouse. Its second-floor gallery wraps around the building, sheltering a vitrine, or display window, on the ground floor.

The next structure is a vivid pink shotgun double with dark green trim and a gabled front. A shallow eave projects forward from the facade, shading the stoops. The proportions of this shotgun house blend perfectly with those of the neighboring cottage, and I realize as I stand under its overhang that, from the vantage point of the sidewalk, it is impossible to tell that this is a shotgun and not a Creole cottage.

The house to the right, though, is the real thing. Its roof ridge is parallel to the street (the shotgun's is perpendicular), and the roof

slopes toward the street, its pitch suddenly becoming more shallow as it nears the sidewalk. The double-pitched roof is common among Creole cottages, and I have been told that the flattened pitch at the front helps carry rainwater away from the house.

I encounter a second Creole cottage as I continue walking toward Burgundy Street. This one is raised higher off the ground than the first one and is larger and deeper. I notice that there is enough room under the roof for a half-story of livable space, illuminated by a pair of tall, narrow dormers.

At the fifth house, I encounter a highly uncommon version of the Creole cottage-house type—a

six-bay cottage appearing to be a double sidehall Creole cottage. Present are elements that express more than one style. The home has a Greek Key door surround with small dentils over the door, hinting at Greek Revival but with drop-lap siding, scalloped running trim, and quoins attributable to the Italianate. It's a puzzle, but I conclude that the growing American influence on the Creole city shaped the house's floor plan and its stylistic expression.

The last visible house on the street is a three-bay cottage, a sidehall version of the traditional Creole cottage. Unlike the original, which would have had no interior halls, this one has a hallway down one side, no doubt an Anglo introduction. Next to it, a white masonry and stucco wall conceals a house from view, but greenery spilling over it makes me think the wall also conceals a lush garden. Nails atop the wall signal "No trespassing" in no uncertain terms.

2000 block of Dauphine Street

THE BLOCK: The 2000 block of Dauphine Street, on the odd-numbered or north side of the street, between Frenchmen Street on the east and Touro Street on the west. Situated in the Marigny Triangle area, the block is near Washington Square, where the community gathers at holiday time for caroling.

THE HOUSES: Nine houses dating to the nineteenth century, including Creole cottages, sidehall shotguns, a two-story townhouse, and double shotguns. Almost all are situated with their front walls right at the sidewalk, as was the custom in the urban environment of the early to mid-nineteenth century.

ANATOMY OF THE BLOCK: I start at the corner of Touro and Dauphine and walk east toward Frenchmen. The double shotgun at the corner seduces me with its color scheme, milled brackets, and fancy gable window. However, the most intriguing elements I see may be the sidewalk bollards in front of it, which presumably protect the building should errant drivers cross over the curb. They are intricately inlaid with tile, a mosaic of faces and bands of unexpected colors.

To the right, I find a Creole cottage with a steeply pitched roof and two tall and narrow attic dormers. It isn't easy to tell always if Creole cottages are doubles or singles, because even singles had two front doors, so this one is anybody's guess. I am thrilled to see an old-style slate roof on this cottage, as few survived the hailstorm of 2000 and Hurricane Katrina in 2005.

A few steps closer to Frenchmen Street, I am standing in front of a sidehall shotgun in the Eastlake style, the third house on the block. It has turned columns and frilly spandrels, as well as carved moldings and details on the door and window trim. From the front, I think the house is modest in size, but then I realize it has a camelback.

Another sidehall shotgun appears next door. The Greek Key trim around the entry suggests that this house is older than its Eastlake neighbor, dating perhaps to the middle of the nineteenth century. I note, however, that it has Italianate-style arched-top windows in addition to its Greek Revival features. Undoubtedly, it was built as one style was going out of vogue and the other coming in.

The adjacent salmon-colored double shotgun is a trickster. Although it looks head-on like a bracketed shotgun from the late nineteenth century, the facade masks an earlier Creole cottage, visible in the side-gabled roofline. In all likelihood, the shotgun facade came later, when owners decided to "update."

Another shotgun and two more Creole cottages appear before I reach the last house on the block, a two-story townhouse with a scattering of Greek Revival elements. Thanks to its corner location and its second story, it offers terrific views down Frenchmen Street and over the tree tops of Washington Square.

600 block of Spain Street

THE BLOCK: The 600 block of Spain Street, on the odd-numbered or east side of the street, between Royal Street on the north and Chartres Street on the south. The colorful block is located in Marigny Rectangle close to the river and around the corner from the Cake Café and Bakery, a cozy place to wait out the rain on the weekday afternoon I visit.

THE HOUSES: A collection of four nineteenth-century houses, two shotgun doubles and two Creole cottages, which front onto Spain Street. On both ends of the block, two-story buildings serve as bookends for the lower-scale residences in between.

ANATOMY OF THE BLOCK: I begin my walk at the corner of Spain and Royal, walking south toward the river. Anchoring the corner here is a two-story with a gallery on the second level wrapping around both the Royal and Spain sides. It's hard to say whether it has a Spain or Royal address, as French doors offer entry on both facades. Turned columns support the gallery, which is ringed with a fancy cast iron railing.

Immediately past the corner building is an Eastlake double shotgun. This is definitely a house to appreciate on foot, because the magnolia trees in front of it on the sidewalk make it difficult to see otherwise. I see that it has a porch across the front and a full retinue of Eastlake details, including turned columns, an elaborate frieze, and decorative millwork of all varieties. The owners were clever enough to use color to emphasize certain features, like the banding created by the drop-lap siding and the raised panel on the front door.

The house next door to the Eastlake beauty is also a double shotgun but in the Italianate style. This house sits much closer to the sidewalk so there's no room for a front porch, just the stoops that are ubiquitous in our older neighborhoods. I stand awhile, enjoying the grace of the arched window and door tops as well as the richly detailed brackets under the eave overhang.

Narrow, tall Creole cottages like the one that comes next are becoming harder and harder to find, even in our Creole neighborhoods like Marigny and Tremé. Just two bays, or openings, wide instead of the more traditional four, this glowing, golden cottage has a tall, narrow dormer and elaborate chimney, both of which draw the eye upward and make the house seem even taller than it is. Is it just me, or does this house look like a giant slice of delectable lemon cake?

A four-bay Creole cottage occupies the spot next door to the lemon-cake house. It's painted a restrained shade of purple and still has a fresh-paint sheen on the drop-lap siding and dark green shutters. I don't know for sure if the small gable-ended building with the red door to its right belongs to this cottage or not, but odds are it was once a garage that was modified for another use.

The tangerine-hued two-story building at the corner makes a dramatic endnote to the block. It faces Chartres Street, so only the side is visible from Spain, but that's enough! Its vivid colors and lovely cast iron balcony add immeasurable charm to the corner, and I can just imagine how the river looks from those upstairs windows.

Faubourg St. Roch

Faubourg St. Roch was added to the National Register of Historic Places in 1994 under the name New Marigny Historic District. Few use that name locally, but there was good reason for the nomenclature. The new district combined areas encompassed by Faubourg Nouvelle Marigny, Faubourg Franklin, and Faubourg Daunois.

The St. Roch district is bounded roughly by North Tonti Street on the north, St. Claude Avenue on the south, the Press Street railroad tracks on the east, and St. Bernard Avenue on the west. Oak-lined St. Roch Avenue serves as the core of the neighborhood and its prime thoroughfare. The boulevard is lined with historic homes and anchored on the north end by St. Roch Cemetery, with its white-washed walls and votive chapel. On the south end, the St. Roch Market, currently closed, is testimony to earlier days when city markets were common.

Of the three Creole faubourgs combined into the district, Faubourg Nouvelle Marigny was the oldest, established by Bernard Xavier Philippe de Marigny de Mandeville as an extension of Faubourg Marigny when demand in the older faubourg outstripped supply of land. Surveyor Joseph Pilié devised the plan for the new faubourg in 1809 and filed it in 1819.

As early as 1818, city surveyor Jacques Tanesse devised a plan to subdivide the Daunois family plantation (formerly the Brewery) into a new development to be called Faubourg Daunois.

A little later, in 1826, Pilié devised a plan for the development of Faubourg Franklin at the behest of landowner Nicholas Destrehan.

Since Hurricane Katrina in 2005, a cultural district has developed along St. Claude Avenue and its side streets, featuring artists' studios, galleries, and a variety of off-beat venues that add to the mix of businesses along the thoroughfare.

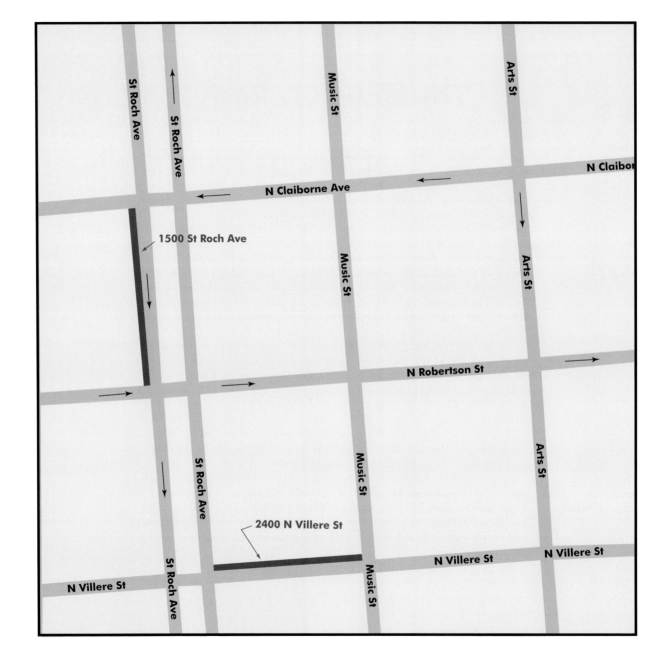

The 1500 block of St. Roch Avenue

THE BLOCK: The 1500 block of St. Roch Avenue, on the even-numbered or west side of the street, between North Claiborne Avenue on the north and North Robertson Street on the south. These bounding streets serve as major thoroughfares for traffic heading to and away from the North Claiborne Avenue bridge over the Industrial Canal. Though cars whiz by on both bounding streets, the 1500 block of St. Roch Avenue remains tranquil.

THE HOUSES: A collection of ten structures, nine of them shotgun houses and the tenth a commercial car repair shop. I count two single shotguns, two sidehall shotgun singles, and five double shotguns (one with a camelback). House styles range from Italianate to Craftsman to Neoclassical Revival.

ANATOMY OF THE BLOCK: The National Register listing for New Marigny indicates that about two-thirds of the historic district's houses are shotguns; therefore,

the 1500 block of St. Roch Avenue scores big since all of its houses fit into one shotgun house type or another.

I start my walk at the corner of North Robertson and walk north, picking out similarities and differences among the collection. The first house is a very simple single in a mildly Craftsman style. Siding obscures its details, but its overall form and character are unmistakable.

The next house is a Craftsman double with much more visible detail—exposed rafter tails, complex entry door units with sidelights and transoms, post brackets in the front-facing gable, and flared trim on the gable window. I note the pattern of glass panes in the transoms over the doors and see that it is echoed in the gable window.

To its right is a sweet single, pink like a nectar soda, with an Italianate-style arched-top window and door and a side addition with a fancy gable. Even though the front gable is small, it

is embellished with a window and decorative millwork.

The fourth house appears to be an Italianate sidehall shotgun that has lost its front porch but gained a Craftsman gable treatment. I don't think its stylistic identity crisis detracts from its overall appeal; it just makes it interesting. Who knows? Maybe the 1915 hurricane blew off the original roof, and the owners decided to replace it with something more *au courant* at the time.

The neighboring Italianate double has all of its details still intact, including brackets and cornices over the windows and door. The mustard-colored sidehall to its right could have been built at the same time by the same builder, considering the similarities between the millwork details and brackets on the two houses.

The seventh house, a blue double closer to North Claiborne, has a camelback, but I can't quite put my finger on its style. I think it may be because the facade has

been altered by the removal of the original columns and, it seems, reconfiguration of the roof over the porch.

Immediately to its right, a meticulously maintained Italianate double gleams. Many of its notable features are highlighted by the use of red paint as an accent. A little more color in the gable would bring out the beauty of its window, sunbursts, and running trim.

I am almost at the end of the block when I reach the last shotgun, a Neoclassical Revival double with a low, wide roof dormer and stout wood columns atop brick pedestals. This owner understands the importance of color placement to underscore detail, for I see that the porch windows with their striking round tops are outlined in lively terracotta color.

The 2400 block of North Villere Street

THE BLOCK: The 2400 block of North Villere Street, on the odd-numbered or north side of the street, between Arts Street on the east and Music Street on the west. On the day I visit in early 2009, several houses have been commandeered for use as installations associated with the Prospect 1 citywide art exhibit. KK Projects art studio and gallery, sponsor for the installations, is immediately across the street.

THE HOUSES: Six houses from the nineteenth and twentieth centuries, three of which are part of the art installation. I don't know exactly how some of them became cultural attractions, but I find the layering of their present-day incarnations over their past lives utterly fascinating.

ANATOMY OF THE BLOCK: I begin at the corner of Music Street and walk east, stopping first at a single shotgun with a long wing extending to the left. The house faces North Villere, but could just as easily have a front door on the other street. It looks like a fence is being installed. Posts are up, but only a tall iron gate is present so far. For a minute, I consider the possibility that this gate—superfluous without a fence—is part of a sly art installation. It isn't, of course, but it could be.

The second house, however, is most definitely artfully manipulated. Cat's claw vines creep up the sides, over the roof, and drop down the front of the cottage. Front doors are flung open to reveal the interior, where a spiral iron stair reaches upward through the ceiling. Long poles with cloth on the ends pierce the roof and structure from every direction. Whatever the artist intended, I can't help thinking of the martyred St. Sebastian, riddled with arrows.

The sidehall shotgun next door leans precipitously toward the pierced house. I've seen enough of these neglected houses that I have trained myself to look past the decay and appreciate what remains, like the slate roof and the faded millwork. However, one thing I am certainly not used to seeing is the prow of a rowboat projecting through a front window, as I see here.

An installation named the *Safehouse* is adjacent. I have seen photos of the white house and its giant bank-vault door, but nothing beats seeing it in person in the context of the block. Something about its clean, white body and the shiny metal vault door makes it especially arresting, almost clinical.

A few steps farther on, a Neoclassical Revival sidehall shotgun stands straight and plumb, unlike the boat house or even the listing corner storehouse across the street. All of its details are intact, making it the perfect foil for the three ravaged houses on the block. It may not be part of the contemporary art installation, but its round, tapered columns; elaborate gable window; modillions over the entry; and dentils on the gable rake boards are just art in another form.

The last "house" facing North Villere really isn't a house at all but a handsomely detailed, two-story garage at the rear of the shotgun house facing Arts Street. Living space above the garage features a columned balcony cantilevered out over the sidewalk plus deep eaves and exposed rafter tails. Most appealing is the wide, low dormer window filled with small square panes of stained glass in a glorious array of colors and translucencies.

Bywater

The Bywater neighborhood was named to the National Register of Historic Places in 1986 after its active neighborhood association petitioned the state of Louisiana for inclusion. The district is bounded roughly by North Villere Street on the north, the Mississippi River on the south, the Industrial Canal on the east, and Press Street on the west.

Like many other New Orleans neighborhoods, Bywater was once the site of riverside plantations that were eventually divided up by their owners for redevelopment. The first was the De Clouet plantation, broken into lots and streets according to a plan by Barthelemy Lafon starting in about 1809. Between 1809 and 1834, when deputy city surveyor Charles F. Zimpel's map of New Orleans was printed, most of what is now Bywater had been subdivided into faubourgs, including Faubourg Cariby, Faubourg Daunois, Faubourg de Lesseps, Faubourg Montegut, and Faubourg Montreuil. According to research by the Greater New Orleans Community Data Center, the six faubourgs were known collectively as Faubourg Washington.

As property became available for purchase, Creoles, Irish, Germans, and Italians quickly settled it in succession, and churches were built to serve the new residents. In 1912, however, one of the area's assets, the eighty-acre Ursulines Convent dating to 1826, was demolished in order to construct the Industrial Canal (or Inner Harbor Navigation Canal, its formal name).

Today, Bywater is home to a cadre of music clubs, restaurants, galleries, and cafés but still maintains its primarily residential character. On one Saturday each month, the Bywater Arts Market fills the Mickey Markey Playground, which serves as a neighborhood recreation spot and dog park between markets.

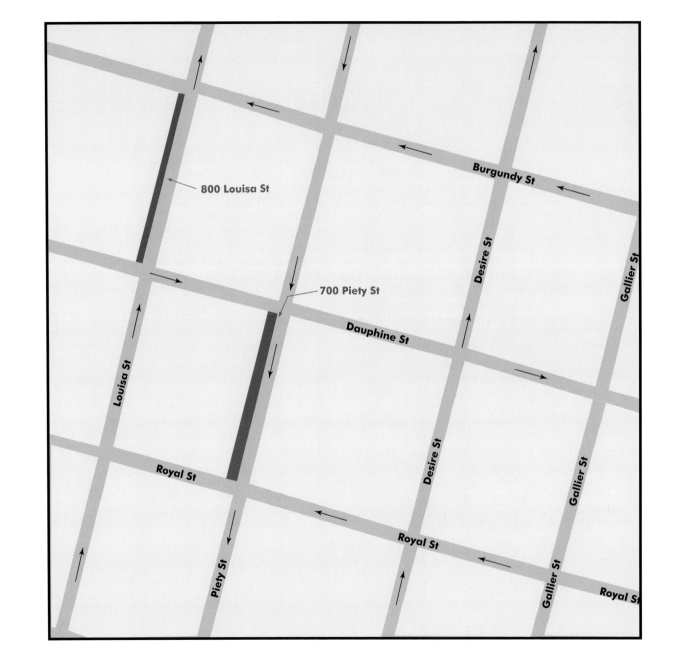

The 800 block of Louisa Street

THE BLOCK: The 800 block of Louisa Street, on the even-numbered or west side of the street, between Burgundy on the north and Dauphine on the south

THE HOUSES: An assortment of house types and styles, including several sidehall shotguns, a frilly double with a camelback, and other variations on the shotgun theme. A corner commercial building anchors the corner of Burgundy. The earliest styles are late Greek Revival and the most recent Art Deco, suggesting the block was developing from the 1850s all the way through the 1930s.

ANATOMY OF THE BLOCK: I start at the corner of Dauphine Street and walk north, passing up a two-story corner building and a Neoclassical Revival single to reach a handsome Greek Revival sidehall. It has a simple entablature and parapet, marked by modest corbels and modillions, which are not bold enough to trespass into Italianate territory.

The next house is a mocha-colored sidehall shotgun with a low, wide dormer; Corinthian columns; and Neoclassical Revival proportions. It occupies a wide lot, and as I keep walking, I see that it has a rear addition plus side and rear porches that are stylistically different from the facade. Instead of Neoclassical Revival details, the side and rear porches feature turned columns, open friezes with spindles and piercework, and curlicue spandrels. The effect is stunning, but I am confused. Was the later Neoclassical Revival house outfitted with porch details of the earlier Eastlake style, or did an Eastlake house get a Neoclassical Revival facelift later in life?

The fifth house is an Italianate single shotgun, painted olive with vivid blue shutters. Because the front wall of the house hugs the sidewalk, there is no room for a porch or steps, so the front door is recessed in a small alcove, framed by pilasters and a segmental arch at the sidewalk. A dash of orange paint has been applied to the finials and recesses of the brackets, echoing the colors of the nasturtiums blooming in the sidewalk garden the day I visit.

My next stop is a grand house on a double lot with robust crape myrtles in the front yard between the porch and iron fence. As handsome as the trees are, they make it hard to see the home's details, but I manage to pick out a few, like the running trim on the gable rake boards, a colorful stained-glass gable window, Tuscan columns on the front porch, a side wing on the left, and a wonderful iron fence, seemingly completely intact. I make a note to revisit in the winter when the crape myrtles have dropped their leaves.

The next house, a double camelback, reprises the exuberant Eastlake trim I spotted on the side and rear porches of the house down the block. Here, I am able to study the millwork up close and note the elaborately carved trim on the window and door surrounds as well as the stained-glass gable window with vents on either side. I also notice jigsaw cutwork embellishments, turned columns, spindles in the frieze, even appliqués at the top of the columns. No surface has been spared adornment.

At the corner, the 1930s-era L. E. Koffskey building features stucco walls and display windows. Whatever Koffskey purveyed in the past, today there is an assortment of chairs in the window. I realize after I get home that I might have been able to verify the building's construction date if only I had checked the tiles inlaid in the sidewalk at the entrance. I'll do it on my next trip.

The 700 block of Piety Street

THE BLOCK: The 700 block of Piety Street, on the even-numbered or west side of the street, between Dauphine on the north and Royal on the south. Across the street is Mickey Markey Playground, which hosts the Bywater Arts Market once a month. Nearby is a former post office (now housing a recording studio and apartments), as well as a variety of corner stores and restaurants.

THE HOUSES: An assortment of six houses in a variety of types and styles, including a sidehall shotgun, a few double shotguns, and a Creole cottage. Several have early Greek Revival details. Like the neighborhood in which they are located, many of the houses express the quirky playfulness of their residents.

ANATOMY OF THE BLOCK: I start my walk at the corner of Royal and walk north toward Dauphine. The double shotgun that I encounter first looks more like an artist's installation than a home, with its wind chimes, plants, tiki torches, and patio table and chairs. I'm pretty sure the stuffed (as in taxidermy) deer on the front porch is genuine, and judging from the red ball covering the tip of its nose, I conclude it was drafted into service for the holiday season.

I next encounter a sidehall shotgun house with Greek Revival detailing such as dentils on the roof fascia and over the entry and Greek Key door and window surrounds. I note the elliptical transom, a design detail I also associate with a house of the era. But wait a minute—what are Ionic columns doing resting atop half-columns of cemented boulders? That's a Craftsman element, not Greek Revival!

A double shotgun next door has a hipped roof, Greek Key surrounds on the doors, and cornices over the openings. I spot the elliptical transoms again, too.

The fourth house, a Creole cottage, wears Mexican weavings in its half-glass doors to provide privacy for the residents. I devise a story in my head. This must be a double converted to a single residence, since the hangings on both doors have the same pattern. Is it? I am so used to seeing houses around town with cryptic codes on their facades that I almost miss this home's Katrina tattoo, a mark left by a search and rescue squad after the storm.

A cheerful yellow Greek Revival double with blue shutters follows. It features a hipped roof, Greek Key door surround, elliptical transom, and highly unusual doors I believe are original to the house.

What's up with the dried vines draping across the facade? Did the residents install them? What do they signify?

The last house before the commercial building at the corner of Dauphine is another double shotgun with a hipped roof. Although it doesn't have a distinguishing feature like boulder half-columns, a stuffed deer, or dried vines on the facade, it fits right in with its neighbors.

Holy Cross

Holy Cross is both a national and local historic district, added to the National Register of Historic Places in 1986 and regulated by the Historic District Landmarks Commission. The district is bounded roughly by St. Claude Avenue on the north, the Mississippi River on the south, Jackson Barracks on the east, and the Industrial Canal on the west.

Most of the area where Holy Cross is now located remained agricultural land until the mid-1800s, when eastward expansion of the city primed its development. The Brothers of the Holy Cross established a boarding school for boys on the site of the Reynes plantation in 1859, giving the area its name. Development continued unabated until the early 1920s, when the Industrial Canal was built on the former site of the Ursulines Convent, separating Holy Cross from the main body of the city.

The neighborhood is home to many historic buildings, including a wealth of nineteenth- and twentieth-century shotgun houses and a scattering of landmarks like St. Maurice Church, the Holy Cross School building, and the two landmark Doullut steamboat houses.

Even though the neighborhood is built atop a natural levee of the Mississippi River (and therefore on "high ground"), it flooded during Hurricane Katrina when floodwalls on the Industrial Canal collapsed to the north, unleashing a tidal wave of water into the neighborhood. More water flowed in when levees along the Mississippi River-Gulf Outlet washed away. Because of the devastation of the Lower Ninth Ward area north of Holy Cross, a "Look and Leave" order was issued after the hurricane, barring residents from staying overnight in either neighborhood. The order wasn't lifted until May of 2006, preventing recovery efforts from starting in earnest until that time.

Today, Global Green, the Sierra Club, the Neighborhood Empowerment Network, the National Trust for Historic Preservation, the Lower Ninth Ward Center for Sustainable Engagement, the Preservation Resource Center, and a host of other nonprofits, private sector businesses, and individuals have assisted the Holy Cross Neighborhood Association as it spearheads neighborhood recovery efforts.

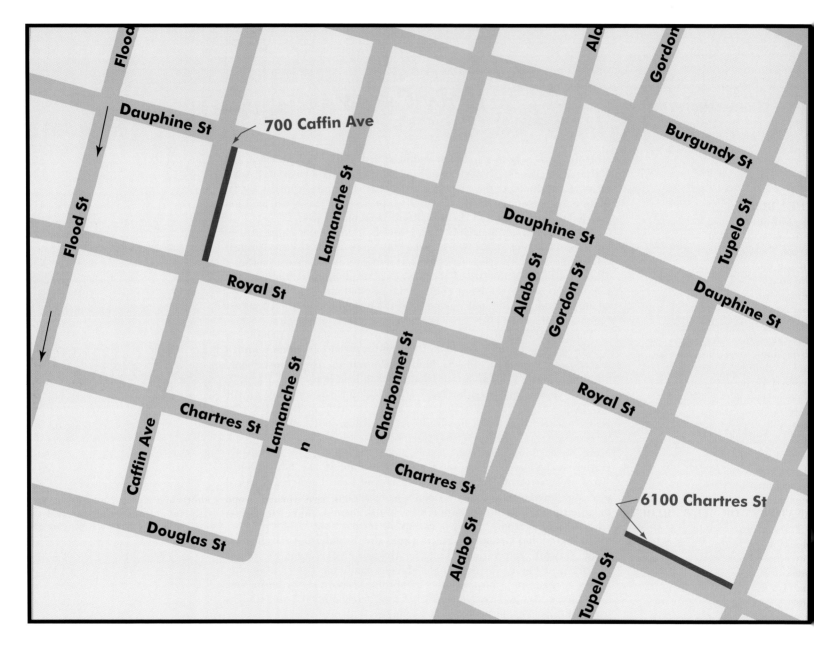

The 700 block of Caffin Avenue

THE BLOCK: The 700 block of Caffin Avenue, on the odd-numbered or east side of the street, between Dauphine Street on the north and Royal Street on the south. St. Claude Avenue, the center of commerce for the area, is just a few blocks to the north.

THE HOUSES: A collection of five shotgun houses, including three single shotguns, one sidehall, and a double. Though each has evolved differently over time, it is very possible that the houses were built at about the same time and once shared distinguishing characteristics. Four of the houses here have been repaired since Hurricane Katrina and seem to be occupied. A fifth house is under renovation.

ANATOMY OF THE BLOCK: I start at the north end of the block at the intersection of Caffin and Dauphine and walk south toward Royal. The first house is an Italianate sidehall shotgun and has been restored. It has arched-top openings, floor-to-ceiling windows, drop-lap siding, quoins on the corner boards, and turned columns. The columns surely extended all the way to the porch decking originally but now sit atop brick pedestals, likely an alteration made when the bottom of the columns rotted out.

As lovely as these elements are, the frieze and gable steal the show. The frieze consists of an arched piece of wood in-filled with turned spindles. It's a rare configuration but an ingenious way of underscoring the arched tops of the windows and door casing. The gable displays a tiny stained-glass window, frilly running trim along the rake board, and a lacy medallion at the peak.

At first, I think the house next door is a Craftsman shotgun because of its wide, low overhang resting on short, flared columns atop brick pedestals. The rounded-arch entry ensemble includes a door and sidelights, also a twentieth-century feature. But when I walk a few more steps and look at the right side of the house, I see it has a semihexagonal bay and a frieze just like the one on the first house. The bay has two turned wood columns and a fancy, half-glass front door, both unmistakably Italianate. I decide the house was originally an Italianate single that was remodeled in the early twentieth century.

The cheery yellow house next door is quite obviously related to the first two. Here again I see the interesting frieze, turned columns, floor-to-ceiling windows, and fancy gable. There's no stained-glass window, but I do note an intricate shingle pattern.

The fourth house has no columns or frieze, just wrought iron supports. But don't I see a tiny remnant of running trim on the gable rake board? Perhaps the similarity of this house to its neighbors has been disguised by the alterations made to it.

I reach the last house on the block and am thrilled to see it is under renovation. It's been altered—vinyl siding applied, millwork removed, and windows shortened—but retains an historic imprint from the arched-top windows and running trim on the gable rake board. I wish I could see what's behind the vinyl siding; I wonder if the workmen plan to remove it.

The 6100 block of Chartres Street

THE BLOCK: The 6100 block of Chartres Street, on the odd-numbered or north side of the street, between St. Maurice Avenue on the east and Tupelo Street on the west. Nearby landmarks include St. Maurice Church, built in 1857, and Jackson Barracks, established in 1834.

THE HOUSES: Seven homes, including a ranch house, three double shotguns, a sidehall shotgun, a single shotgun, and an immense corner storehouse. Demolition appears to have occurred recently between two of the shotgun doubles, leaving a vacant lot.

ANATOMY OF THE BLOCK: I start at the corner of Tupelo at a red brick ranch house overgrown with weeds and apparently abandoned. It's impossible to walk on the sidewalk because of the overgrowth, but I am heartened when I see a Sweet Autumn Clematis vine blooming bravely in the thicket.

Walking east toward St. Maurice, I encounter a double shotgun with a brick facade. I can tell from the fancy window and millwork in the gable that this house once looked much different from how it appears today and that it likely dates to the late nineteenth or early twentieth centuries. It is separated from the third house by a wide side yard shaded by blooming crape myrtles and surrounded by a traditional iron fence.

The house behind the fence is an Eastlake sidehall shotgun, under renovation on the day I visit. I spot a full array of details, including turned columns, quoins, drop-lap siding, spandrels, and a frieze. The frieze in particular attracts my attention because it is composed entirely of piercework squares instead of a combination of turned spindles and piercework, as is more common. Cornices atop the windows and door add extra height and dimension.

A wonderfully colorful double appears next. It's Eastlake, too, with turned columns and a frieze with turned spindles. Dramatic millwork flourishes grace the gable and complement the other details.

To its right is a vacant lot. I can almost see in my mind's eye the little single house that used to stand there. Though the house was not especially intriguing, its absence leaves a gap in what would otherwise be an intact block.

A few steps more and I am in front of an Italianate double shotgun with arched-top windows, milled brackets, and cornices with crowns over the windows and doors. The roof is asymmetrical; the overhang on the left side is much deeper than on the right. I have seen roofs like this before, but I have never been able to come up with a good explanation for them.

One step closer to the corner is a tidy single shotgun with a giant cactus in front. It's shadowed by a corner storehouse, the former home of Dubose Pharmacy, now vacant and in disrepair. Despite its condition, I can see it has all the right elements to be a handsome addition to the block and the neighborhood if it were repaired and restored.

Arabi

Arabi is a small riverside town in St. Bernard Parish immediately downriver of Jackson Barracks and just outside Orleans Parish. Like riverside neighborhoods in adjacent New Orleans, Arabi was once the site of plantations that were eventually subdivided and was originally a suburb of the city.

Arabi's development did not begin in earnest until about 1880, after New Orleans banned stockyards within its city limits. The action prompted the Crescent City Stockyard and Slaughterhouse to relocate downriver to Arabi and spurred related residential development in the area. When the American Sugar Refinery (now Domino) was built in 1906, the increased commerce sparked still more residential growth and the construction of Arabi's now historic homes.

Landmarks in Arabi include the historic sugar refinery and two circa-1850 plantations: Le Beau and Cavaroc, the latter on the grounds of the refinery.

Although Arabi occupies the high ground close to the river in St. Bernard Parish, it flooded during Hurricane Katrina when floodwalls and levees failed catastrophically. The area continues to rebuild and repopulate.

The 400 block of Angela Street

THE BLOCK: The 400 block of Angela Street, on the even-numbered or west side of the street, between Douglass Street on the north and Bienvenue Street on the south. The block is located in the Old Arabi Historic District, which was added to the National Register of Historic Places in 1998 in recognition of its architectural merits and association with the history of Arabi. Houses on the even-numbered side of the street back directly onto Jackson Barracks, a military post dating back to the 1830s.

THE HOUSES: A half-dozen single-story houses including three single shotguns, one sidehall shotgun, a double shotgun, and a bungalow. Styles reflect tastes of the late nineteenth century (Eastlake) and early twentieth (Craftsman and Neoclassical Revival).

ANATOMY OF THE BLOCK: I start at the corner of Bienvenue and head north, visiting first a turquoise single shotgun on a wide lot. I admire its steeply pitched roof, fish-scale details in the gable, and a three-part gable window with stained glass. I look down the block and see the configuration repeated in several more houses and wonder if the same person built them all.

Its neighbor is a taupe-colored shotgun double. Here proportions and elements are typical of the Neoclassical Revival style. The roof dormer is wide, with an accent on the horizontal rather than the vertical. I note the wider door and window openings, characteristics suggesting to me that this house was built a little later than some of the other houses on the block.

A plaque on the front identifies the house as belonging to the Old Arabi Historic District.

The blue sidehall shotgun a few steps closer to Douglass Street has the same steeply pitched gable with fish scales that I saw on the first house I visited. The glass in its front door is etched in an elaborate pattern. I see a Katrina tattoo on the shutters and imagine that the owners decided to leave it there as a badge of courage.

A dazzling white single shotgun follows. It has a side gallery that begins several rooms back and extends to a side entry. Here, again, I see the gable with its stained-glass attic window, this time inscribed with the letter "N." Just under the gable, I notice handsome egg-and-dart-style molding.

The fifth house on the block is a yellow Craftsman bungalow, in the midst of a renovation. Trucks are parked in front and workmen come and go as I take pictures. Next to it, at the corner of Douglass, I study a single with a side gallery like the one on the white house. I note it has the same gable and egg-and-dart molding. It also has a generous side addition extending into the side yard. Down the side street, the brick buildings and walls of Jackson Barracks frame the view.

The 500 block of Friscoville Avenue

THE BLOCK: The 500 block of Friscoville Avenue, on the odd-numbered or east side of the street, between Poplar Street on the north and Bienvenue Street on the south. The block is located in the Friscoville Street Historic District, added to the National Register of Historic Places in 1998. Development of the district began in 1906 after the grounds of the Le Beau Plantation were laid out into streets and blocks. Just a block or so away from the target block is the Arabi Food Store, a neighborhood institution and home of the seafood mufaletta, and the LeBeau Plantation house.

THE HOUSES: Seven twentieth-century houses, some still in recovery mode after Hurricane Katrina.

ANATOMY OF THE BLOCK: I start at the north end of the block, at the corner of Poplar, and work my way south toward the river. The first house is under renovation. It's a two-story, but I find it hard to peg its style. I am thinking that the downstairs porch might have been closed in at some point because the picture window doesn't seem quite right.

It is next door to another two-story house with a more distinctive personality, an up/down duplex that I think was probably a single-family home once. I note Craftsman details like the porch railing, "snake's mouth" rafter tails extending past the upstairs porch overhang, and battered (gently tapered) columns. The more I look at the two houses together, the more I think they might have once been twins before one of them was altered over time.

The third house is a 1935-era, single-story cottage behind a white fence, in perfect condition and displaying a seasonal wreath. The wreath picks up the color of the terracotta ridge tiles on the roof and sets off the house's subtle color scheme. The spider-web transom over the front door is a telltale sign of the period in which the house was built.

As I continue, I encounter a Neoclassical Revival double shotgun with Tuscan columns that are round, slightly smaller at the top than the bottom, with a simple capital. This house is under renovation, too, and I think how lucky the owners are to have so much original material to work with, such as the floor-to-ceiling windows and three-part gable window.

A two-story, blond brick apartment building comes next. It's built slab on grade, and instead of grass in front, there is concrete. This intrusion may have replaced an older building or perhaps someone sold off their side lot at some point to allow its construction.

The sixth house is a white cottage with a low, wide dormer and an asymmetrical facade. Cast iron columns and railings adorn the front porch but are likely replacements of what was originally there.

The last house, closest to the river, is set far back from the sidewalk and shaded by palms. This one has been totally restored since the storm and features classic Craftsman elements like battered half-columns on brick pedestals and a front door with sidelights. I note the green canvas awnings—instead of the metal ones I often see—that protect the front windows from the bright afternoon sun. A wide brick path, extending the full width of the steps, invites vistors up onto the porch.

SECTION III
ACROSS THE RIVER

High ground along the Mississippi River has always been at a premium, whether located on the river's east bank or west bank. And although the French established La Nouvelle Orleans on the east side, it wasn't long before settlers were also taking advantage of the natural levees along the river on the opposite side.

Crossing over the Crescent City Connection from downtown New Orleans today, it's difficult to visualize the small communities that hugged the river both upstream and downstream 150 years ago. But Algiers, McDonoghville, Mechanikham, Gretna, Marrero, and others all shared the high ground and easy commerce that came from their riverside locations.

Algiers in Orleans Parish and Gretna in Jefferson Parish have particularly interesting streetscapes composed of historic homes and buildings. And they have another asset in common: ferries that connect directly to the foot of Canal Street. The ferry ride provides convenient access to both communities and offers dramatic views of the New Orleans skyline in the course of the journey.

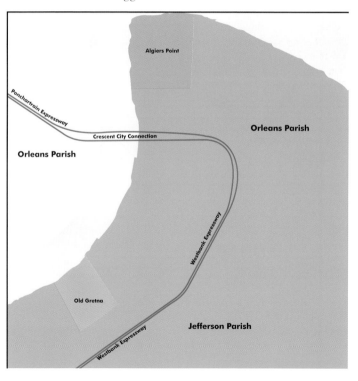

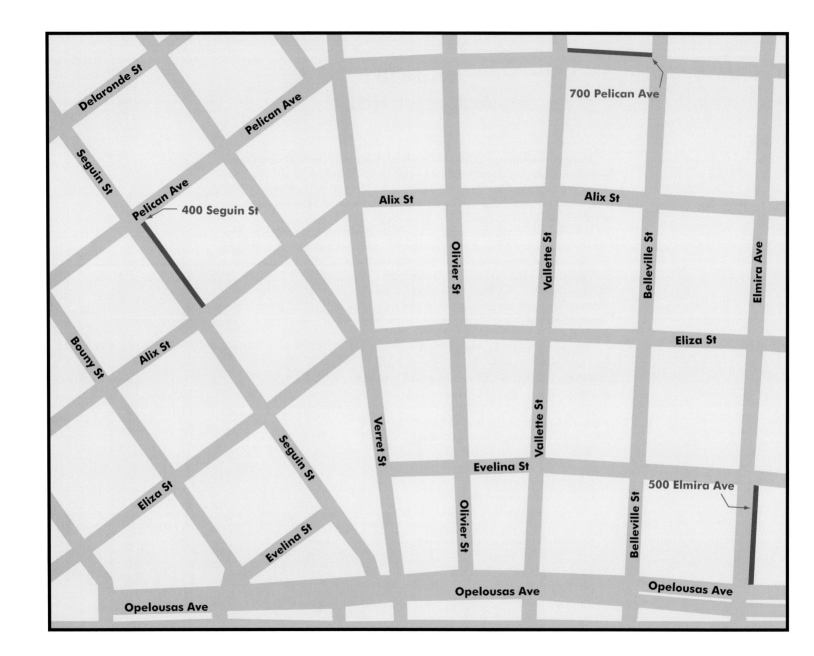

Algiers Point

Algiers Point is a local and National Register Historic District on the "Westbank" of New Orleans, across the Mississippi River from and linked to the French Quarter and Central Business District by the Algiers-Canal Street Ferry (in operation since 1827). Although it is separated from "Eastbank" New Orleans by the river, it is nonetheless an integral part of the city and within the boundaries of Orleans Parish. As for the "Westbank" and "Eastbank" nomenclature, never mind that the Canal Street Ferry travels from west to east to reach the Algiers Ferry landing, Algiers Point is still considered to be on the Westbank!

The Point is bounded by the Mississippi River on the north and west, by Atlantic Avenue on the east, and by Newton Street on the south (historic district boundaries vary). Before it was annexed to New Orleans as the Fifth Municipal District in 1870, Algiers was a bustling town with its own governance and industries. It was built on the site of the Duverje Plantation, which was subdivided about 1839 by its owner, Barthelemy Duverje, according to a plan by Alan d'Hemecourt. It grew rapidly thanks to an ever-expanding dry-docking industry, shipbuilding, and eventually the construction of the railroad. The Duverje Plantation home, built in 1812, eventually served as the Algiers Courthouse.

A devastating fire in 1895 destroyed nearly half of Algiers—two hundred homes and almost ten square blocks—making way for the existing courthouse as well as new homes in fanciful late-nineteenth-century and early-twentieth-century revival styles. Landmarks include the courthouse, several churches, historic school buildings, and the 1907 Hubbell Library, built with funds from Andrew Carnegie.

Today, the Algiers Point Association looks after quality of life in the neighborhood and sponsors an annual home tour in October. The springtime counterpart to the tour is the Old Algiers RiverFest, which draws thousands to the Westbank of the river to sample New Orleans food, music, and crafts.

The 700 block of Pelican Avenue

THE BLOCK: The 700 block of Pelican Avenue, on the even-numbered or north side of the street, between Belleville Street on the east and Vallette Street on the west. On the opposite side of the street is one of the neighborhood's oldest remaining houses, a Greek Revival center-hall home built in 1848. The Hubbell Library is located at the Belleville corner of the block.

THE HOUSES: A group of seven homes, including five that are two stories tall. Styles include Greek Revival, Italianate, and Craftsman.

ANATOMY OF THE BLOCK: I start at the corner of Vallette Street and walk east, pausing to study the pink house on the large corner lot filled with white angel trumpets and fuchsia bougainvillea. I can't really categorize its type and style, but it is evident that this owner likes to garden, for a row of potted plants lines the street edge of the brick sidewalk.

The next-door neighbor has an extraordinary porch that wraps all the way across the front and down one side on both the first and second floors. Box columns—five top, five bottom—support the gallery and roof. The color scheme is adventurous—yellow siding, white trim, pale lavender sash, purple shutters, and a robin's egg blue door. It sounds wild, but it somehow fits the personality of this house perfectly.

The third house on the block is a New Orleans raised-basement house with a central stairway to its two upstairs units. The wide, low dormer on the roof and flared wood columns atop brick bases signal the home's Craftsman style. My favorite element is the saw-toothed brickwork at the bottom of the porch balustrade. It's subtle, but it tells me someone took extra care to distinguish this house from its peers.

Now I stand in front of an Italianate double-gallery house with an ornate cast iron fence. This house must be a survivor of the 1895 fire, for its architectural style dates back two or three decades prior to the event. Some of its finest features are the Corinthian columns on the first level, the milled brackets on the second, and what looks to me to be a thirty-foot-tall sweet olive in the front yard. Ah! Now I see it—a marker on the fence states the build date was 1871.

The house to its right is a single shotgun and one of just two one-story houses on the block. The two remaining tall windows on its facade have an Italianate segmental arch at the top, leading me to think that the shortened front door may have had a transom in this shape at one time.

If I were driving instead of walking past the double next door, I would not see its Italianate windows and doors, drop-lap siding, or quoins. Nope—I would have been taken in by the angle brackets under the roof eave, the exposed rafter tails, the clusters of columns atop brick bases, and the flared gable window. "Craftsman!" I would have proclaimed and gone on my way.

A tall, narrow house with Tuscan columns occupies the corner at Belleville. I can't tell from looking at the front if the tall masonry base is original to the house or a later addition. It doesn't matter, really, for what gives the house character are its Tuscan columns and beautifully detailed front gable.

The 400 block of Seguin Street

THE BLOCK: The 400 block of Seguin Street on the even-numbered or east side of the street between Pelican on the north and Alix on the south. Neighborhood venues like the Dry Dock Café and the Crown and Anchor Bar are just around the corner, a few steps from the ferry landing. In the other direction is the grand Holy Name of Mary Church, which faces an inviting triangular green. On the day I visit, a movie crew has set up operations in the church parking lot and is filming inside the Old Point Bar.

THE HOUSES: A collection of five houses, four of them double shotguns, in styles ranging from Eastlake to Neoclassical Revival to Craftsman.

ANATOMY OF THE BLOCK: I begin near the corner of Pelican and walk south past the side of the corner house to take a look at the first house facing Seguin. It is an Eastlake double, but not a typical double. In fact, it suggests a center-hall because the millwork between the two center columns is arched, as if to frame an entry. I look closer, though, and I see that the house is an asymmetrical double: a two-bay single unit on the left and a sidehall unit on the right. Clever!

The owner has used color to accentuate details like the banding of the facade's drop-lap siding and the panels on the front doors. Now I see something else intriguing—sawn balusters in the porch railing. From a distance, these look like turned balusters, but in fact, they are flat boards cut into shapes to mimic turned balusters and are seen rarely in urban neighborhoods.

It's hard to tear myself away, but next door a Craftsman double beckons. Here I see hallmarks of a Craftsman-era house, like flared wood columns atop brick pedestals, a low porch overhang with exposed rafter tails, and angle brackets in the gable.

But wait! What are Italianate quoins doing running up and down the corner boards? And why are the tops of the windows and the transoms over the doors arched, as if they belonged to the Italianate era? For that matter, what are floor-to-ceiling windows doing on a Craftsman house? I realize I have been duped. This house may have a 1920s-era facade, but underneath, it's older, closer in age to the two Eastlake shotgun doubles to the right of it. You could say it had a facelift.

The two neighboring doubles share many features, including half-glass doors, floor-to-ceiling windows, decorative crowns or cornices over the openings, and lots of fanciful millwork. However, they aren't twins. Since millwork patterns differ—the turned columns are an example—I conclude they weren't built by the same person but were meant to harmonize nonetheless.

I reach the corner of Alix and study the only single-family home on the block and its Neoclassical Revival features. Its columns aren't turned as on the Eastlake houses nor are they flared and boxy as on the Craftsman impostor. They are round Tuscan-style columns, narrower at the top than at the bottom. The windows on this house are shorter than on neighboring houses and display complex glass patterns in the top and bottom sash—diamonds, spider webs, and sunbursts. Barely visible in the frieze atop the columns are graceful garlands and swags, applied in relief. Looking down the right side of the house, I see the bell tower of Holy Name of Mary Church over the tree tops.

The 500 block of Elmira Avenue

THE BLOCK: The 500 block of Elmira Avenue, on the odd-numbered or west side of the street, between Eliza on the north and Evelina on the south. An immense two-story Italianate building anchors the corner of Eliza, across from Louie's Corner Bar. Holy Name of Mary Church, Tout de Suite Café, and Rosetree Glass Studio are within a radius of a few blocks.

THE HOUSES: Eleven houses, including three single shotguns, a cottage, a two-story corner store-house, and six double shotguns (some converted to singles). Styles include Greek Revival, Italianate, "New Orleans Bracket," Eastlake, and Craftsman.

ANATOMY OF THE BLOCK: I start at the corner of Evelina and walk north. The first house is a sidehall shotgun dressed in Eastlake finery. Plenty of froufrou-like turned columns, an open frieze with turned spindles and piercework, a half-circle attic window, and decorative gable shingles. This house is a dead ringer for an historic home, but I have a foggy memory of it being built to historic standards a few years before Katrina. Ditto for the bracketed double shotgun next door—do I remember that it is the second of three skillful reproductions? It has large milled brackets and floor-to-ceiling windows, making it fancy but more understated than its Eastlake neighbors.

An Eastlake single follows and I admire its paint colors and their placement, a grayish green for the body, green sash on the floor-to-ceiling windows, and a darker green applied to the narrow recessed bands in the drop-lap siding. The color variation produces a low-contrast stripe, which adds dimension and personality.

The first three houses on the block were all raised high and set back from the sidewalk, but the fourth is lower. It's a shotgun double with a shallow-pitched hipped roof that sits close to the front property line, leaving just enough room for a front porch and a sidewalk planting bed.

The Craftsman double shotgun that I see next features exposed rafter tails, angle brackets, clusters of short wood columns, brick column bases, multipaned front doors flanked by sidelights, and a gable window with flared trim and dazzling green and blue stained glass. The Craftsman single on its right echoes many of the features.

I am now standing in front of the seventh house on the block. My guess is that it is the oldest, based on its cottage form and mild Greek Revival style. It has three windows with a door on the far right, making me wonder if maybe it could have begun its life as a double.

A double shotgun in the "New Orleans Bracket" style is the eighth house. The term was coined by Lloyd Vogt, who used it in his book *New Orleans Houses* to refer to shotguns with cantilevered porch overhangs and milled brackets.

The ninth house, a Craftsman double converted to a single, features unusual columns. Instead of wood, the clustered half-columns here are made of brick just like the pedestals supporting them.

I pass a Craftsman single and reach a mammoth two-story corner storehouse at the intersection of Eliza. Its most striking feature is the row of Italianate floor-to-ceiling windows wrapping across the front and down both sides of the building on the second floor. The fact that these are full-length windows tells me there was once something there, like a balcony, which was accessed through the tall windows.

Old Gretna

Gretna is an historic community in Jefferson Parish directly across the river from the Lower Garden District of New Orleans. The early residents of Gretna knew a thing or two about the importance of establishing their community on high ground, and so they built as close to the river as they could, atop the natural levee formed by thousands of years of sediment deposited when the river overflowed each spring.

Although the city of Gretna was not incorporated until 1913, a plan for its precursor, Mechanikham, was commissioned by Nicolas Noel Destrehan in 1836 and laid out by surveyor Benjamin Buisson. Buisson's plan for Mechanikham consisted of a grid of streets accented by a wide boulevard now known as Huey P. Long Avenue. Today its shady neutral ground terminates at the 1907 Jefferson Parish Court House, now Gretna City Hall.

Critical to the success of the fledgling Mechanikham was the 1838 establishment of a second settlement, Gretna, by the St. Mary's Market Steam Ferry Company. The two communities were eventually combined with the Jefferson Parish portion of McDonoghville and then incorporated as the city of Gretna.

Gretna encompasses a variety of neighborhoods, including the Gretna Historic District, added to the National Register of Historic Places in 1985. The district is centered on City Hall, the ferry landing, and the city's business district and is bounded roughly by First Street on the north, Ninth Street on the south, Amelia Street on the east and Dolhonde Street on the west. According to the National Register, the district is especially notable because it comprises the largest and most "architecturally rich" collection of historic buildings in all of Jefferson Parish.

Events like the weekly farmers' market, monthly art walks, and the annual Gretna Heritage Festival make Gretna a great place to live and to visit.

The 1300 block of Adams Street

THE BLOCK: The 1300 block of Adams Street, on the even-numbered or east side of the street, between Virgil Street on the north and Romain Street on the south. Although the block is not located in the official Gretna Historic District, its wealth of historic homes certainly makes it a candidate for a street walk. Across the street is a shady grove of mature cypress trees and a linear green space, flanking railroad tracks.

THE HOUSES: Six houses from the late nineteenth century and early twentieth century, including two Eastlake single shotguns, a Craftsman corner storehouse, a bracketed double shotgun, an L-shaped shotgun with a wraparound porch, and a Queen Anne cottage.

ANATOMY OF THE BLOCK: I begin my visit at the corner of Virgil and walk south toward Romain. My first stop is a light green corner storehouse built in the Craftsman style. The commercial side is on the left and a large window with protective roll-down shutters confirms that this half of the building was indeed used for commerce at one time. True to the Craftsman style, it has deep eaves and post brackets with pyramidal caps.

As I walk a few more steps, I see the residential counterpart to the commercial space. In contrast to the functional doors at the corner, the entry doors to the residence are fancy, all glass with sidelights and a detailed transom. I admire a wide side yard, filled with blooming azaleas and other flowering plants.

On the opposite side of the yard, I stop to admire an Eastlake single shotgun with an exuberant array of millwork. Turned columns, an elaborate frieze with piecework panels and spindles, spandrels, and cornices over the front openings are on display. Next door, the third house is another Eastlake single, this time set in the midst of a stand of cypress trees. With its restrained ornamentation and shaded setting, it evokes the feel of a peaceful country cottage.

My next stop is a shotgun double, converted to a single. How can I tell? Four openings across the front would usually signal two units, side by side, each with a door and window to the front porch. But here there is a door on the far left and three windows to its right, suggesting the second entrance became obsolete at some time and was replaced with a window.

Oh, what a treat comes next! In form, this is a simple shotgun with a side wing at the rear, but the wonderful wraparound porches—across the front, down the side, and across the rear wing—make it something glorious.

At the corner of Romain stands a stately white cottage with plentiful porches and a bay on the left. It's the grande dame of the block and features Queen Anne styling. I note Tuscan columns and a gabled roof over its side bay, ornamented with shingles and a half-round stained-glass window. Louvered shutters shade its openings from the afternoon sun and a low stone fence (or concrete cast to look like stone) imparts additional stature.

The 700 block of Huey P. Long Avenue

THE BLOCK: The 700 block of Huey P. Long Avenue, on the odd-numbered or east side of the street, between Seventh Street on the north and Eighth Street on the south, in the Gretna Historic District. The block is entirely residential, with the exception of the Mt. Zion Baptist Church at the corner. A block to the south, Thomas Jefferson Magnet High School faces the grand boulevard and businesses appear to the north, clustered around City Hall. Some of the monumental oaks on the avenue's neutral ground are hung with holiday ornaments when I visit during Christmas season.

THE HOUSES: Five shotgun singles and one double in varying styles. Low, white wood fences separate several of the houses from the sidewalk and some sections are decorated with holiday garlands.

ANATOMY OF THE BLOCK: I start at the corner of Seventh and walk south, stopping at the Mt. Zion Church to decipher its construction date. A stone on the front says it was dedicated in 1975, but it looks much older to me because of the striated bricks that were used, some decorative brickwork on the facade, and its crenellated square towers. I snoop and find an older cornerstone on a side elevation and it confirms my guess; the church was founded in 1906 and rebuilt in 1915. Perhaps the first church burned? Or might it have been destroyed in the 1915 hurricane?

Three nearly identical shotgun singles are next. They're all about the same height and width and elevation off the ground, with front porches and columns. Each has a gable facing the street, and I notice that all of the gable windows are semicircular, though there are minor design differences. Each facade features a walk-through window and a half-glass door. The middle house still has its original louvered shutters. Two of the singles have round, tapered columns, but the third house's columns are turned wood. From the styles and proportions of the houses, I would call them all Neoclassical Revival and believe they date from about 1900 to 1910.

I notice the fourth house is very different from its neighbors to the left. It's a single shotgun like the others but has lower ceilings so it looks "shorter" from the outside. This house is solidly in the Craftsman category, as evidenced by its blocky brackets and door with sidelights. Even so, it blends well with its neighbors because of its scale and massing and because of the wood fence that ties all four houses together visually.

As I continue walking, I encounter a double shotgun. Its proportions—tall ceilings and steep-pitched roof—suggest to me that it is closer in age to the first three shotguns on the street than the Craftsman house next door.

To its right is a high-style Eastlake single shotgun on a wide corner lot. It has all the details so highly prized for this style, including turned wood columns and balustrade, an open frieze with spindles and piercework panels, spandrels, quoins on the corner boards, louvered shutters, arched-top windows, and fish scales in the gable. When I turn the corner, I see that the house is L-shaped and has a side porch featuring all the same millwork details as the front.

The 300 block of Lavoisier Street

THE BLOCK: The 300 block of Lavoisier Street, on the even-numbered or west side of the street, between Third Street on the north and Fourth Street on the south. The block is located in the heart of the Gretna Historic District just two blocks away from the neighborhood's grand thoroughfare, Huey P. Long Avenue, which hosts an art walk every month.

THE HOUSES: The block is entirely residential and features five double shotgun houses in styles ranging from Eastlake to Craftsman. Most are set back a short distance from the sidewalk and a few have attractive fencing and front gardens.

ANATOMY OF THE BLOCK: I start at the corner of Third Street and walk north, stopping in front of a taupe-colored Craftsman double with dark red double doors. I take note of the many features characteristic of the Craftsman style, like tapered box columns atop stone pedestals, exposed rafter tails, and simple post brackets on the gable. I see that the trim around the gable window flares out toward the bottom, another Craftsman hallmark.

A Neoclassical Revival double shotgun follows. Its facade features round, tapered columns atop short pillars. The same material visible on the pillars, likely a form of concrete cast to look like stone, also sheathes the foundation and the low fence dividing the front yard from the sidewalk. The facade displays a distinctive window design, which consists of a single pane of glass in the bottom sash topped by a decorative arrangement of panes in the top sash.

I move on and am about to study the third house on the block when I notice that the gray house has a side-gabled portion behind the gable-fronted facade. I've seen this condition in other old neighborhoods, and it usually means an earlier house—a cottage of some kind, set far back from the street—gained a new facade and more square footage years after it was first built.

Now I turn my attention to the Neoclassical Revival double in the third spot on the block. Like its neighbor to the left, it features handsome windows. These are round-topped with a "spiderweb" transom and a top sash featuring an elongated diamond pattern. Again, the bottom sash is a single pane of glass. Another distinguishing feature here is the clipped or flattened gable on the roof.

Now I am standing in front of a white house with a diamond-patterned gable window and tapered circular columns. I notice that this house has one set of steps in the middle, leading directly to the two entry doors. Elsewhere on the block, doors are on the outside of the facade with windows in the middle. The variation isn't especially remarkable, but it reminds me how even subtle variations can animate a streetscape.

The rose-colored Eastlake double at the north end of the block serves as a delicious visual dessert at the end of a satisfying walk. Crisp white trim contrasts with a dark rose body and green black shutters to create a delectable composition, artfully complemented by the home's colorful garden.

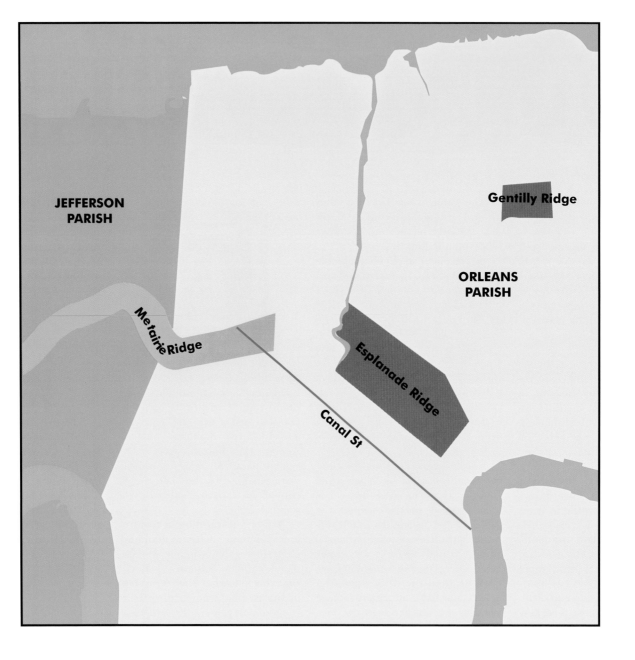

Section IV
Along the Ridges

The natural levees of the Mississippi River weren't the only high ground in New Orleans suitable for habitation. In fact, the entire area was veined with a number of bayous, which created natural levees of their own and were prized as sites for development.

Chief among these waterways was Bayou Sauvage (later renamed Bayou Gentilly), which stretched across the area from along what is now Gentilly Boulevard to Bayou St. John. There, it intersected Bayou Metairie (formerly Bayou Tchoupitoulas), which ran along what is now Metairie Road. Bayou St. John once had a spur that extended southeast from its current termination and became the site of an important Native American portage.

Over the course of thousands of years, the banks of these bayous were built up by sediments deposited whenever the bayous overflowed their banks. These sediments coalesced into the high, firm ground we know today as the Gentilly, Esplanade, and Metairie ridges.

Gentilly Ridge

Several neighborhoods flank Gentilly Boulevard, the oldest of which is Gentilly Terrace and Gardens on the north side of the thoroughfare. South of the boulevard are Edgewood Park and Lower Gentilly.

Gentilly Terrace was added to the National Register of Historic Places in 1999 for its extensive collection of California-style Craftsman bungalows. The area's boundaries are roughly Mirabeau Avenue on the north, Gentilly Boulevard on the south, Peoples Avenue on the east, and Spain Street on the west.

Best known as New Orleans' first automobile suburb, Gentilly Terrace's "new world" origins extend back to 1727 when Bienville granted Mathurin de Dreux a tract of his choosing in reward for service. Noting competition for high ground adjacent to the Mississippi River, Dreux chose instead a tract of high ground along a bayou, which he named Bayou Gentilly (an extension of Bayou Sauvage). In the early 1800s, the Dreux family divided their land and sold it to various buyers, including Charles Williams Hopkins. Hopkins established the Hopkins Plantation where Gentilly Terrace and Edgewood Park stand today. In 1885, he sold the north half of the plantation to Charles Dietz and the south half to Dennis Sheen.

In 1909, after several more transactions, the Dietz tract was purchased by Michael Baccich and Edgar deMontluzin who soon thereafter established the Gentilly Terrace Company with partner Edward Lafaye. Their development relied on a suburban model never before seen in New Orleans. Provisions were made for automobiles, and the California Craftsman bungalow, the newest craze in American residential architecture, was touted as the most desirable house type (though revival style houses weren't forbidden). Lot elevation was augmented by soil excavated to build roads, confirming the marketing slogan "Where Homes are Built on Hills."

The Sheen tract south of the boulevard became Edgewood Park, developed in the 1920s and 1930s. Though not now a historic district, it was surveyed after Hurricane Katrina and deemed eligible for listing on the National Register. Bounded roughly by Gentilly Boulevard on the north, I-10 on the south, Peoples Avenue on the east, and Clematis Street on the west, it features a collection of Craftsman bungalows and raised-basement houses with a scattering of other styles popular in its era. West of Edgewood Park is Lower Gentilly, developed between the 1920s and 1940s. Homes are mostly single family in the Craftsman, Colonial Revival, English Cottage, and Spanish Revival styles. Despite widespread flooding during Hurricane Katrina, many houses closest to Gentilly Boulevard stayed dry, thanks to their elevations.

The 4400 block of Arts Street

THE BLOCK: The 4400 block of Arts Street, on the even-numbered or west side of the street, between Lombard on the north and Gentilly Boulevard on the south, in the Gentilly Terrace district. The block has a mix of early-twentieth-century house types and styles, including several Craftsman bungalows. There are a few ranch houses, a clue to the fact that the neighborhood did not finish developing until after World War II. All are on wide, terraced lots with drives.

THE HOUSES: Eleven houses including a terrific collection of Craftsman bungalows, plus a few mid-twentieth-century brick dwellings.

ANATOMY OF THE BLOCK: I start my walk at the corner of Gentilly Boulevard and walk north, passing up the first two brick houses to get to the first Craftsman bungalow on the block. I check for details. Let's see . . . Are there wide overhanging eaves? Most certainly, especially at the front porch. A multiple gable roofline? Why, yes, there is a lower gable in the front and a taller one in the back. And I also note a porch spanning the full width of the house, its overhang supported by short, tapered box columns atop tall brick piers.

Next door I encounter a pink house with even more Craftsman characteristics. The chimney on the right side of the house pierces the wide overhang of the roofline and is dotted with protruding boulders, a favorite California Craftsman device. The house next door to it is its mirror image, right down to the lattice covering the gable vents. On both houses, the porch is over to the side rather than in the middle, yielding the asymmetrical facade, which is another Craftsman identifier.

I skip the brick ranch house that follows and move on to the next bungalow. Its multiple gables, low-pitched roof, and deep eaves with brackets earn it high points on the Craftsman scorecard. Stout stucco columns flare widely, enhancing the California Craftsman flavor.

The next two houses are paragons of the style. The first one has the same low-pitched roof I saw on other houses, plus a low, wide dormer that accents the horizontal character of the roof and house. The neighboring house has a similar roof, but its dormer is actually gable-ended, adding just a little height.

I pass over a small red brick ranch house to admire the house on the corner. The red barrel tiles on the roof and red tile path and steps try their best to convince me this is a Mediterranean Revival house. But I see too much Craftsman in the details and proportions, starting with the roof's low pitch and dominating character.

Okay, so what if some of the openings on the front have arched tops? Look at the house from the side, note the overhanging roof and the eave brackets, check out the trio of windows in the side gable, and observe the low, wide shed-roofed dormer. Then tell me if it's Craftsman or not.

The 4600 block of Music Street

THE BLOCK: The 4600 block of Music Street, on the even-numbered or west side of the street, between Carnot on the north and Lombard on the south, in the Gentilly Terrace district.

THE HOUSES: Ten houses, including Craftsman bungalows, a Colonial Revival, a quasi-Tudor Revival, and a Neoclassical Revival. The mix drives home the point that revival styles were popular in the first decades of the twentieth century and a variety of different versions were often employed in newly developed neighborhoods like this one. A couple of houses at the Carnot end of the block appear to be in recovery from Hurricane Katrina, but the remainder of the block is lovingly cared for. Since Gentilly Terrace was New Orleans' first automobile suburb and designed to accommodate motorized vehicles, most houses occupy wide lots and have driveways.

ANATOMY OF THE BLOCK: I begin at the Lombard end of the block and walk north toward Carnot. My first stop is a tidy Colonial Revival house, gray, with a split-level floor plan and red shutters to provide a pinch of color. Dormers accent the cottage roof. A white two-story house with a red tile roof is next door. It has been altered, but it is basically an "American Foursquare" with an off-center front porch. The adjacent Colonial Revival house has the same red tile roof as the foursquare, plus fan transoms over both the front windows and the front door.

Moving on, I stop in front of a coffee-colored bungalow with red accents on the door and window sash. One term often applied to bungalows is "low slung," and I think this house makes clear exactly what that means—low to the ground (you don't see the foundation because the siding covers it) and wide, with a low-pitched roof and ultrawide, low dormer. Details like the brick half-columns with post ends, grouped post columns, and an asymmetrical facade design are all high-style Craftsman details.

Next comes a kelly green bungalow with a front gable, a feature that gives this house added height especially in contrast to the house next door. I know the facade has been modified—probably an open porch was enclosed on the right side—but the dramatic, asymmetrical roofline is intriguing nonetheless.

I don't know how to describe the beige and brown stucco house next door, but then I decide it's okay to meet an architectural mystery every now and again and move on to the light green bungalow next door. Unlike many of its neighbors, it has a symmetrical facade. I note the geometry of the intersection of the front-gabled main roof and the side-gabled porch roof, an innovative practice used in Craftsman design.

I am finally in position to study the two-story salmon-colored house with red roof and shutters. It has a porch off to one side, covered by a highly articulated roof with exposed rafter tails. Post columns rest atop flared brick half-columns to support the porch roof. I see a white wicker chair on the porch and imagine how the homeowner must love to sit there in the shade and look at the array of flowerbeds—almost like wild flowers—that cover the terraced lot. Who wouldn't?

The 4700 block of Spain Street

THE BLOCK: The 4700 block of Spain Street, on the odd-numbered or east side of the street, between Mirabeau Avenue on the north and Carnot Street on the south, in the Gentilly Terrace district.

THE HOUSES: Eleven houses representing many types and styles, including English Cottage, Craftsman, Colonial Revival, and Mediterranean Revival. There is even a brick ranch house, undoubtedly built decades after the others. A couple of the houses on the block are still being renovated and another one or two are unoccupied or for sale. But most, including those on the opposite side of the street, appear to be well-loved homes. All are set back from the street on terraced lots and feature driveways, an amenity that the developers advertized and a thoroughly modern consideration at the time.

ANATOMY OF THE BLOCK: I begin at the corner of Mirabeau and walk south, passing the little house with the English Cottage-style roof, which is under renovation at the corner. Next door to it is a pink up-down duplex with screened-in porches on the left side for both the upstairs and downstairs units. I see that the entry to the downstairs unit is on the left of the house, through the porch, but that the upstairs unit has a separate entry on the right side of the facade.

A Colonial Revival cottage comes next, its roof punctuated by a pair of tall dormers. It is followed by a Mediterranean Revival cottage in a warm-toned brick with a handsome red tile roof. The entry is recessed in a shallow alcove, marked by a round-topped arch supported by two Solomonic columns. I notice more arches on the right side of the house, encircling the open porch.

The fifth house on the block is a split-level with an entrance to the garage on the left and to the living area on the right. I suspect that it, like the green house on its right, has been altered to the degree that it's difficult to discern its original character.

I catch my breath and realize I have been rushing past the first houses on the block. It's because I am impatient and want to reach the glowing white villa with red barrel-tile roof that is located mid-block. I want to spend a long time savoring its design and massing.

What to look at first? The house has almost too many delicious features to describe, an open porch on the left balanced by a closed living area on the right, with a terrace in between. The arches on the left side porch repeat, at a smaller scale, on the right. I see the twisty Solomonic columns again as well as three gables in varying sizes extending forward at varying depths.

The eighth house, to the right of the villa, is its stylistic antithesis: a symmetrical, restrained, two-story Colonial Revival home. Here I note a muted color palette and see that everything is properly square instead of arched and twisted. It is a perfect counterpoint to its voluptuous and extravagant neighbor to the left.

Filling out the block are a Mediterranean Revival bungalow with double clipped gables and stucco arches, a wide center-hall with a gabled front and transitional styling, and a blonde brick ranch house.

The 4100 block of Clermont Drive

THE BLOCK: The 4100 block of Clermont Drive, on the odd-numbered or east side of the street, between Gentilly Boulevard on the north and St. Vincent Street on the south, in Lower Gentilly. Because the block is so close to the natural ridge along Gentilly Boulevard, the houses here did not flood during Hurricane Katrina.

THE HOUSES: Eight houses all reflecting the floor plans and styles that were the rage between the 1920s and 1940s. There are three split-level houses with garages, plus examples of Mediterranean Revival, English Cottage, and Colonial Revival.

ANATOMY OF THE BLOCK: I begin at Gentilly Boulevard and walk south toward St. Vincent Street. The first house is a split-level with garage. Its living area is raised a few feet above grade and accessed via an entry porch on the left side. I notice the pilasters flanking the front door and pairs of Tuscan columns supporting the roof over the porch.

To its right is a white house, which seems to combine a few different styles. The dominant feature is a stucco wing, which extends forward from the main body of the house and has a gabled facade inset with a circular window. I feel as though it has a vague Mission Revival shape to it. The main body of the house, by contrast, has a Colonial Revival cast, with a bay on the right side and a fan-shaped millwork embellishment over the second-story window.

The third house is a tidy cottage with a red tile roof, a recessed entry, and a gable-fronted wing that extends forward on the right side. The lot is terraced, so it's necessary to climb a step or two before reaching the front steps and entry.

Although the pink house next door does not have obvious Mediterranean Revival features, I nudge it into that category for its stucco facade and series of arches over the door, in the gable window, and on the left side of the facade.

The side arches undoubtedly once rimmed an open porch, which is now enclosed as living space. When I focus my attention on the garage portion, I realize this house is similar to the split-level at the beginning of the walk but in a different style.

The blue house that follows is an ornamented version of a Colonial Revival cottage, with a roof balustrade, dormers with pilasters, and pilasters again flanking the entry door. The columns supporting the roof overhang surely must have once rested on a front porch rather than on cement, so I try to picture the house with the porch restored.

Another split-level, this one yellow, is next door. It's very much like the first house I visited, except for the detailing on the front porch. Here, the roof slope extends in one fell swoop from the ridge of the house to the edge of the porch, and the columns supporting it are square.

I find the block's only English Cottage a little farther on. It has

the steeply pitched, asymmetrical double gables associated with the style, as well as stone work around the entry. The rustic front door is definitive, too: vertical planks of wood with an arched-top and round window.

The last house on the block appears to have been freshly renovated and painted. I try to puzzle out its original appearance—garage doors on the bottom at the right and perhaps an open porch on the left. Whatever the case, the home's cheery colors and perfect condition serve as an excellent reward at the end of the walk.

The 2500 block of Wisteria Street

THE BLOCK: The 2500 block of Wisteria Street, on the even-numbered or south side of the street, between Franklin Avenue on the east and Iris Street on the west, in Edgewood Park. Like Gentilly Terrace to the north, Edgewood Park was built in the automobile era, so most houses feature driveways.

THE HOUSES: A group of nine houses, most with a Craftsman flavor, all one-story. Five are single-family residences with asymmetrical facades, the porch on one side with windows on the other. The doubles are symmetrical, in contrast, but none of them is exactly alike. For all the uniformity of scale and siting of the houses, there are plenty of interesting differences.

ANATOMY OF THE BLOCK: I start my walk at the corner of Franklin Avenue and walk west, first encountering a green house with pink trim and turquoise porch and steps. The porch extends forward from the body of the house on the right side, its roof supported by tapered wood columns atop half-columns of brick. An attic vent in the gable of the body of the house offers ventilation.

Next door is one of the double houses, painted beige pink. It features the same wood-atop-brick column configuration, but its porch stretches the full width of the house so that residents on both sides can enjoy the shade it offers. A brightly colored gable window with elaborate trim adds interest.

A few steps closer to Iris Street, I encounter a second double, this one painted a dark forest green with cream trim. Here, the brick column bases are taller and covered with stucco, and the columns are shorter and stucco instead of wood. The gable features a modest window, but I look closely and see that the trim flairs slightly, one of my favorite Craftsman details.

The fourth house is the glamour girl of the block. Not quite as pink as a nectar soda, she is decked out with high-style Craftsman millwork, including a cluster of small columns atop brick half-columns, vertical boards in the porch and house gable, and an arbor over the walkway to the front porch. The wood columns have applied details and recesses, fancier than the others on the block. But for all of her high style, this house has the same overall form as the other singles on the block—a porch and entry on one side of the house and a room with windows on the other.

The salmon-colored house on the right is also a single. This house introduces a new element to the style vocabulary of the block: the full-length column. Instead of a short wood column resting on a half-column of brick or stucco, this house features a single tapered box column extending from the porch ceiling to the decking. The effect slenderizes the porch's appearance and makes it seem a little taller.

The yellow and green house I encounter next features more new elements, including a double-gabled roof. The house on its right is a symmetrical double with a low porch overhang and exposed rafter tails. Its neighbor is another single, this one with a screened entry porch projecting outward on the left. The very last house is a wide double on a terraced lot, which requires two flights of steps to reach the front porch.

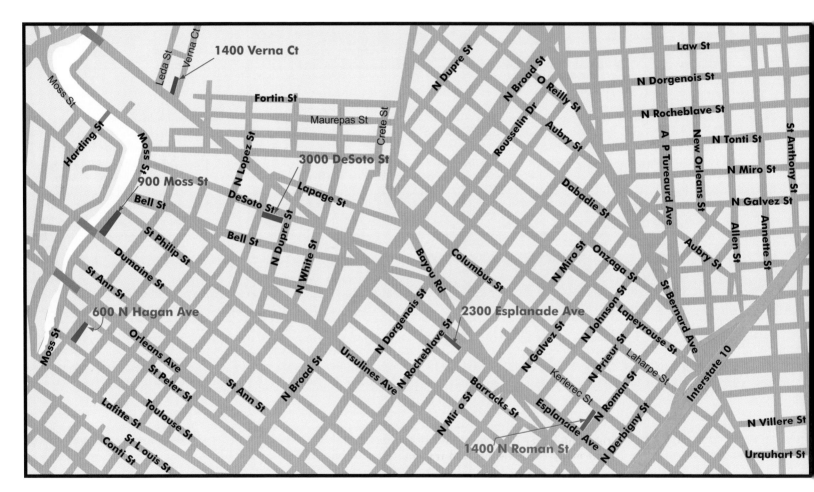

Esplanade Ridge

Esplanade Ridge stretches on either side of Esplanade Avenue, from the north edge of the French Quarter to Bayou St. John. Named to the National Register of Historic Places in 1980, it encompasses three distinct neighborhoods: Tremé, Esplanade Ridge, and Faubourg St. John. The district is bounded roughly by Bayou St. John on the north, North Rampart Street on the south, St. Bernard Avenue/Onzaga Street on the east, and Orleans Avenue on the west.

The district developed gradually as New Orleans grew outward from the Vieux Carré, expanding along a high strip of ground that was once a Native American portage connecting Bayou St. John to the Mississippi River (now the location of Esplanade Avenue). According to the National Register, the district's growth occurred in stages as development stretched ever farther into what had been outlying plantation lands. Faubourg Tremé, closest to the Vieux Carré, represents the first phase of expansion and Faubourg St. John the last.

What the Garden District was to the Americans, Esplanade Ridge was to the Creoles. It was the epitome of their culture's social and architectural expression. The city's Creole elite built grand homes, especially along Esplanade Avenue, as well as Creole cottages, double-gallery townhouses, and center-hall villas. As time passed and the district developed more densely, shotgun houses were added to the mix.

The glorious Bayou St. John serves as a fishing hole, paddling venue, and prime picnic spot for New Orleanians; however, it was far more than that two hundred years ago. Bayou St. John, not the river, was the main water route into the city for more than a century, meaning that many early visitors and traders were introduced to La Nouvelle Orleans from Bayou St. John's waters. Today, walkers, joggers, and cyclists ply the paths alongside its glittering waters daily, even in the hottest months.

The Fair Grounds Race Course has been a landmark in the neighborhood since the 1870s and is one of the oldest continually operating tracks in the nation. It is also the site of the annual New Orleans Jazz and Heritage Festival. Other landmarks include the circa 1800 Pitot House on the banks of the Bayou; the Luling Mansion, formerly the New Orleans Jockey Club; and the Degas House, the Esplanade Avenue home where French Impressionist painter Edgar Degas stayed with family during a visit to New Orleans in 1872-73.

The 1400 block of North Roman Street

THE BLOCK: The 1400 block of North Roman Street, on the odd-numbered or north side of the street, between Kerlerec Street on the east and Esplanade Avenue on the west, in the Esplanade Ridge neighborhood.

THE HOUSES: A quartet of houses of varying types and styles, including a grand Creole cottage, a lacy shotgun, a Craftsman camelback double, and a house of uncertain style. Three are set back from the sidewalk, and the Creole cottage is situated with its facade on the banquette. I am so accustomed to visiting blocks where houses are stylistically related that I find the diversity of house types and styles refreshing.

ANATOMY OF THE BLOCK: I begin my walk close to the corner of Esplanade, where a grand center-hall house occupies the corner lot facing the boulevard. I am nearly mid-block before I reach the first house fronting North Roman, a crisply painted red and white double camelback. Judging by its proportions and the double entry doors, the house likely dates to the early twentieth century. Iron has replaced its original columns, but I can picture Tuscan columns on this house in keeping with its Neoclassical Revival style.

The green house to the right is harder to peg. You can't tell from the front but if you look down the side alleys, you'll see that the house has a dramatic cottage roof line, with an open gallery along the Kerlerec side. How much do you want to bet that this house started life as a Creole cottage before acquiring arched-top windows and other Italianate characteristics later in the late nineteenth century? The changes didn't end then, however, for I see that Craftsman-style columns have been added, no doubt in the early twentieth century. I can read the evolution of the house from standing on the sidewalk and can't help wondering what motivated the successive alterations.

When I look at the petite shotgun single next door, I realize it might offer some clues to how and why the neighboring house developed as it did. I spot the same arched-top openings, the same siding, and even the same little gable-ended projection at the entry. Maybe when the little Eastlake house went up, the neighbors liked what they saw and decided to "update" their old Creole cottage.

The frilly single is dwarfed by the Creole cottage to its right, the last house on the block. The cottage has a stucco facade but wood sides and two well-proportioned roof dormers. Its roof pitch is steep near the ridge and then abruptly flattens over the sidewalk to create what was called an abat-vent. Stucco on the facade is scored to emulate stonework, adding to the monumental character of the house. All indications are that it is an early house, maybe 1830 to 1850.

Then a mystery arises. I realize that the facade is asymmetrical because of a fifth bay on the Kerlerec end of the house. Then I notice something else; the bay sits under its own roof rather than under the main roof of the house, leading me to think it's a later addition and not original to the house. So I study the entry door, which is located in the fifth bay, and my theory is confirmed. It's a half-glass door with small stained-glass panes rimming the central pane, a late nineteenth-century feature. Before I leave, I glimpse the faint ghost of a Katrina tattoo to the left of the entry.

The 2300 block of Esplanade Avenue

THE BLOCK: The 2300 block of Esplanade Avenue, on the even-numbered or west side of the street, between North Rocheblave Street on the north and North Tonti Street on the south, in the Esplanade Ridge neighborhood. It's a tree-shaded block with extra-wide sidewalks, perfect for strolling. It is also the block where the Musson home was located, now known as the Edgar Degas house for the artist's 1872 visit with his Musson relatives.

THE HOUSES: Five large homes, two of which I can confidently describe as mid-nineteenth-century double-gallery townhouses and three more that I am not so sure about. All are two stories or more tall, and the consistent massing gives the block a coordinated look, even if the styles vary considerably.

ANATOMY OF THE BLOCK: I begin at the North Tonti end of the block and walk north, musing on the two houses closest to the corner. I know their back story. They were once a single center-hall home,

which Degas' cousins rented for ten years and where Degas stayed when he visited New Orleans from October of 1872 to the spring of 1873. The house was literally cut into two unequal portions early in the twentieth century, and the smaller portion was moved about twenty feet to the left to create a second house.

Armed with this information, I look through the twentieth-century facade on the corner house, searching for the mid-nineteenth-century form of the original house hiding behind it. I note the frieze that runs below the eave, and I can match it with the frieze on the Degas House on its right.

Without two of its bays, the house that Degas' family rented is no longer a center-hall; it is now a double-gallery sidehall townhouse. You would never guess from looking at it that it had ever been anything but a townhouse. It has all the signature features, like a side entry, galleries at both levels, and walk-through windows.

Wary of how easy it is to be tricked by appearances, I walk toward the third house on the block. It's another handsome two-story home and has a pair of leaded-glass front doors, a bay window with detailed millwork, and a roofline that turns up slightly at the eaves. My instincts tell me this is a somewhat exotic version of a Neoclassical Revival foursquare house, but who's to say it isn't an older house made to look newer?

Neither palm trees nor metal sculptures can hide the grand house on the next lot. Although

I can't see the body of the house because of front yard foliage and art installations, I can see a fabulous roof gable, supported by Ionic columns, above the greenery. Its stylish Neoclassical Revival details include an open pediment, cornice molding, dentils, and a round gable window.

The last house is another two-story sidehall townhouse and is in the midst of being restored. A fresh coat of white paint has been applied to the body and trim and the shutters have been painted dark green. I note a hard-to-find treatment on the facade, a grid of raised wood panels meant to imitate the look of stone work, a device called rustication.

The 3000 block of DeSoto Street

THE BLOCK: The 3000 block of DeSoto Street, on the even-numbered or west side of the street, between North Lopez on the north and North Gayoso on the south, in the Faubourg St. John neighborhood. Esplanade Avenue, with its markets, coffeehouses, and restaurants, is just a block away in one direction, Bayou St. John a few blocks away in another. I visit in December, when the neighborhood celebrates the holiday season with Esplanade Fest and candlelight caroling by canoe on the bayou.

THE HOUSES: A collection of five houses set back from the sidewalk on generous lots. The houses at each end of the block have a strong Craftsman character, a double shotgun mid-block reflects the Neoclassical Revival style, a fourth house has a front gable with a hint of Tudor Revival styling and Stick-style spandrels between the columns, and yet another has an Eastlake feel.

ANATOMY OF THE BLOCK: I begin my walk at the corner of North Gayoso Street and walk north, stopping first at a raised-basement Craftsman bungalow. I notice mitered corners where the weatherboards meet at the corners and unusual porch columns. They are covered in wood siding until almost the top, where stucco takes over. The side-gabled roofline is punctuated by a dormer with a front-gabled roof. And although the dormer exhibits Craftsman details, I wonder if it is original to the house. I would have expected something with a lower profile.

Next door is a rose-colored house with a Tudor Revival gable—stucco with applied boards imitating half-timbering. It has a very steeply pitched roof, exposed rafter tails, and a wraparound porch ringed with Tuscan-style wood columns. The columns are topped with simple wood spandrels that call to mind terms like "Stick style" and "Carpenter Gothic." I make a mental note to show a photo of this house to an expert so I can learn more about it.

An enchanting center-hall cottage is the third house on the block. A semi-octagonal bay projects forward from the main body of the house on the left side and the front porch is located on the right. On the bay, I note rosettes in the corners of the trim, milled brackets in its roof overhang, and a totally original shingle pattern in its gable. On the porch, turned columns and lacy spandrels with running trim command my attention. Queen Anne or Eastlake? I can't decide.

I walk a few more steps to view a highly detailed Neoclassical Revival double shotgun. I take in the stained glass in the diamond-patterned windows, the roof dormer on the right, and the fancy capitals on the porch columns. I notice that the right side and its entry are slightly recessed from those on the left, affording each resident an extra measure of privacy.

The last house is a low-slung, shingled Craftsman bungalow. Everywhere I look on the house, I see original details, such as the multipaned top sash on the windows and the high-style Craftsman portico over the front entry. The pea green color of the window sash against the blue of the body helps accentuate its details. On the left, a wing sits back from the plane of the main body of the house, and I see that its windows are set higher in the wall than elsewhere. Could it be this is the kitchen wing and the windows are set higher to accommodate kitchen cabinets beneath them?

The 1400 block of Verna Court

THE BLOCK: The 1400 block of Verna Court, on the even-numbered or south side of the street, between Marie Street on the north and Esplanade Avenue on the south, in the Faubourg St. John neighborhood. Houses on the even side of the street back onto the Fair Grounds Race Course. I wonder what it would be like to have the Jazz Fest in your backyard, to sit on your porch and listen to the music, to people-watch as fest-goers walk by. There are only a few blocks in the city that would afford such an experience, and this is one of them.

THE HOUSES: An assortment of early-twentieth-century houses in varying sizes and styles. There is no real pattern—one house comes right up to the sidewalk, another is set far back. One has an ample front yard and garden, another has a terraced lot. Yet many features of early-twentieth-century styles, like exposed rafter tails and low, wide dormers, are in abundant supply and help tie the group together.

ANATOMY OF THE BLOCK: I begin my walk close to the intersection of Verna and Marie, and walk south toward Esplanade. I stop first to consider a gray raised-basement house with a hefty square tower, inset with windows. You could watch the horse races (or Neville Brothers) from that tower, I am sure of it! The house still has its terracotta roof, and the residents have wisely picked up on the color and used it to accent the window sash.

Next door, a Craftsman-style house is enlivened by vivid, tropical colors. It has a side-gabled roofline accented by a low, wide dormer. Telltale exposed rafter tails appear in the roof overhang. The left half of the front yard is grass but the right half is a field of sand where I noticed both children's toys and large metal cut-out sculptures.

I walk on to a two-story purple house with intriguing details too numerous to count. Someone has taken a lot of time to get the colors just right, design the perfect garden, and add personal elements. I take a closer look at the gable boards; I think maybe they have been made especially for this house; the pattern of carving is one I have never seen anywhere else. The garden is lush and features a metal orb fountain. Who would think that olive, purple, and salmon would work well together? But they do. The biggest chromatic surprise is blue applied to the underside of the eaves and the porch floor.

After the exuberance of the dragon house (did I forget to mention the dragon sculpture perched atop one of the gables?), I experience the soothing simplicity of the Craftsman double adjacent to it. The roof is side gabled, like the one on the second house on the block, and it has a wide shed roofed dormer. Here, though, the roof extends out beyond the front wall of the house to create a front porch with flared wood columns. Round-topped openings lead from the interior to the porch, which provides a perfect spot for people watching.

The 600 block of North Hagan Avenue

THE BLOCK: The 600 block of North Hagan Avenue, on the even-numbered or south side of the street, between St. Peter Street on the east and Toulouse Street on the west, a block outside the boundaries of the Faubourg St. John neighborhood. With few buildings on the north side of the street, these houses offer an almost unobstructed view of Bayou St. John from their stoops.

THE HOUSES: An intact row of ten double shotguns, which appear to have been built in the early years of the twentieth century, judging from their Neoclassical Revival styling. Rooflines, window types, and gable configurations vary from one end of the block to the other; however, the uniform size, scale, foundation treatment, and metal roofs tie the houses on the block together. The builder could have made each house identical to the others but chose instead to mix and match a palette of elements to animate the composition.

ANATOMY OF THE BLOCK: I study the block from a distance, identifying patterns and repeated elements. Every one of the houses is about the same size and scale; each has two doors, one on the right and one on the left, with two short windows in the middle. Every one has a set of five handsome milled brackets under the front overhang.

I note that rooflines, however, vary from one house to another. There are four houses with front gables, three houses with hipped roofs, and three more houses with clipped gables (a flat area rather than a peak at the top of the gable). Some have dormers, some don't. All appear to have gable windows, though some are covered.

I move closer for a better look and start my walk at the corner of St. Peter, heading west. I see right away that most of the doubles have doors with squared tops, but this one and its twin at the opposite end of the block have doors with rounded tops, just like their windows. Other features this house shares with its twin are stuccoed gables and gable windows composed of multiple panes of stained glass.

The green house next door has flat-topped windows and doors, with a hipped roof and dormer set with low, wide windows. The third house is an amalgamation of elements from the first two houses on the block, with flat-topped doors but rounded-topped windows, a clipped gable, and a low, wide gable window.

And so it goes as I walk toward Toulouse Street. Flat-topped doors and windows with a gable front on one house, flat-topped doors with rounded windows and a clipped gable on the next. The elements, it seems, can be combined in every way imaginable and yet the houses remain in perfect harmony.

The 900 block of Moss Street

THE BLOCK: The 900 block of Moss Street, on the even-numbered or south side of the street, between St. Philip Street on the east and Dumaine Street on the west, in the Faubourg St. John neighborhood. Houses on the block face Bayou St. John.

THE HOUSES: Six nineteenth-century houses including three double shotguns, a sidehall shotgun, a raised center-hall house, and a grand plantation-style home. Most of the houses exhibit features of late-nineteenth-century architectural styles, but the grand plantation-style home expresses the French Colonial style of the late eighteenth and early nineteenth centuries.

ANATOMY OF THE BLOCK: I start out at the corner of St. Philip Street where I find an Eastlake double shotgun with glorious details. There are turned columns and balusters, a spindle frieze, frilly spandrels and running trim, drop-lap siding, quoins on the corner boards, cornices over the windows and doors, louvered shutters, and a fancy triple window in the gable. I almost overlook the sunburst pattern in the gables over the entries! If I were writing a book about Eastlake shotguns in New Orleans, this would be my centerfold.

The next-door neighbor is another fine example of the style and type, though more restrained. The turned elements are present as are the spandrels and quoins, and I see a fanciful seashell pattern in the crown atop the cornices. A large handpainted sign in the front planting bed commands me to "LOVE DUCKS."

The sidehall shotgun I encounter next is a little weathered, but its inherent beauty shines through. All it would take to make it picture perfect would be to remove the shingle siding, then sand and paint the weatherboards. Plotting the makeover, I see something I missed at first—the seashell-patterned crown above the openings. So is this house a single cousin of the double to its left?

Now that I know what to look for, I see that the raised center-hall is another member of the tribe. Here again, I see the distinctive seashell crown as well as quoins and drop-lap siding. The shutters are divided into three vertical parts, exactly like those on the sidehall and the double.

It seems I have discovered three houses with the same stylistic DNA but with different floor plans: two side-by-side hall-less units in the double; a single unit with a hall down one side in the sidehall; and a single unit with a hall down the middle and rooms on either side in the center-hall. Clever!

The diva of the block is known as The Sanctuary, a French Colonial plantation-style house that sits behind a tall iron fence with mammoth posts. The two-story house has a *rez-de-chaussée* at grade with living quarters above. A deep gallery wraps across the front and down two sides, ringed with slender "colonettes" that support the roof above the gallery. Below, stout Tuscan columns built at grade support the second-floor gallery.

The final building on the block is a curiosity, a double shotgun not more than one room deep! The little house makes a quirky footnote to a glamorous block, but then, what house could compete with the diva to its left?

Metairie Ridge

The Metairie Ridge owes its existence to Bayou Metairie, originally called Bayou Tchoupitoulas, an important waterway in colonial times. Today, only a small section of Bayou Metairie exists along the City Park Avenue edge of City Park. But its lagoon-like appearance belies the fact that Bayou Metairie originally intersected Bayou St. John at about Esplanade Avenue and flowed west, past what is now City Park and Metairie Cemetery, through what is now Metairie and out toward Kenner.

Like Bayou Gentilly to the east, Bayou Metairie played an important role in development of the land surrounding it, thanks to the natural ridge it built up over centuries along its banks. High ground was prized in swampy New Orleans, and so Metairie Ridge provided an attractive and hospitable location for development.

Today, Metairie Road follows the ridge and serves as the topographical and commercial backbone of the neighborhoods that flank it.

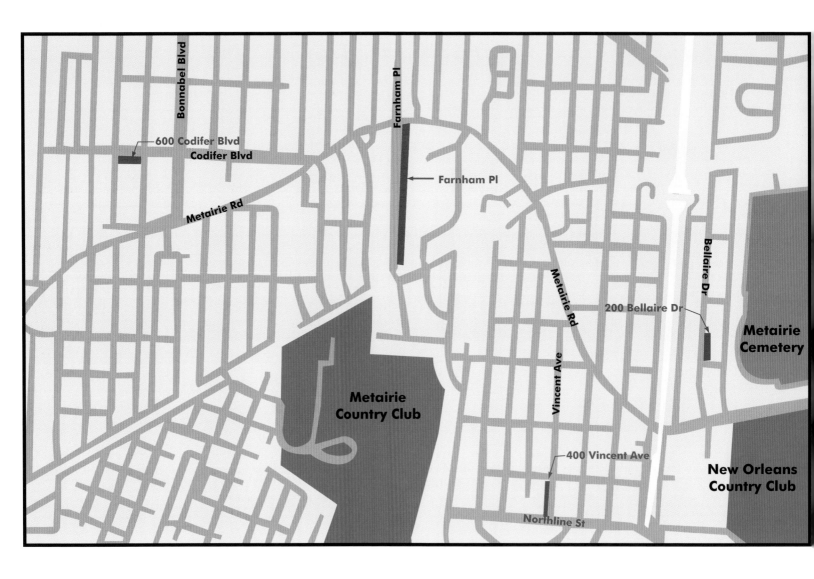

Bonnabel Blvd

Farnham Pl

600 Codifer Blvd
Codifer Blvd

Farnham Pl

Metairie Rd

Bellaire Dr

Metairie Rd

200 Bellaire Dr

Metairie
Cemetery

Vincent Ave

Metairie
Country Club

400 Vincent Ave

Northline St

New Orleans
Country Club

The 200 block of Bellaire Drive

THE BLOCK: The 200 block of Bellaire Drive, on the odd-numbered or east side of the street, between Ethel Lane on the north and Natalie Street on the south, in the Country Club Gardens neighborhood of Orleans Parish. The residential enclave is bounded roughly by the Norfolk Southern Railroad on the north, Palmetto Street on the south, Metairie Cemetery and New Orleans Country Club on the east, and the Seventeenth Street Canal on the west.

Development of Country Club Gardens began after 1924, when a plantation owned by the Friedrichs family was subdivided. Metairie Road bisects Country Club Gardens, separating Maryland, Bellaire, and Fairway drives on the north from Garden Lane and Bamboo Road on the south. Longue Vue House and Gardens is nearby.

THE HOUSES: A baker's dozen of twentieth-century homes ranging from modest wood cottages to immense two-story houses. I count several Colonial Revival houses in brick and wood, a 1970s-era Southern Colonial, two one-story stucco cottages, and a few large houses in styles popular in the 1990s. Many residences within two or three blocks of Metairie Road and its natural ridge remained dry during Hurricane Katrina flooding.

ANATOMY OF THE BLOCK: I begin at the corner of Ethel Lane and walk south toward Natalie. The first house is a well-proportioned two-story brick home in a form repeated frequently on the block. It has a side-gabled roof, three openings across the front at each level, and a rectangular footprint. It loosely fits into the Colonial Revival category, but its front door, which is topped by a pediment, is located to one side, rather than in the center as is traditional.

The second house is a large, new brick residence with a two-story bay on the left front and a grand arched entry. The house to its right appears to be an early split-level house that was modified over time, so that its integral garage has been converted to living space.

A 1930s-era cottage with multiple rooflines and distinctive round-topped openings appears next. The tallest gable features a pair of casement windows and an iron railing. Another new house (or recent remodel) follows. Pairs of round columns on either side mark its entry, and its openings all have rounded tops.

The sixth house may be the best example of the Colonial Revival style on the block, owing to its symmetrical facade, broken pediment with swan's neck detailing, and pilasters flanking the front door. I notice that the windows on the first floor have an "8 over 8" configuration—eight panes of glass in both the top and bottom sash.

I move on to study the next house, but the dense trees in front make it impossible, so I skip to the adjacent two-story brick house with tall columns. It's what I would call a Southern Colonial Revival style, adhering to the basic principles of the Colonial Revival style, but having a roof that extends forward from the front plane of the house, supported by tall columns.

A well-proportioned and detailed newer home follows, then a charming cottage behind a white picket fence. It is the only fence I have encountered on the block, and it encloses a front yard divided into a carefully planned series of outdoor rooms.

Three houses complete the block, one of which is an exemplary Colonial Revival complete with a symmetrical facade, a central entry, a broken pediment over the front door, and flanking pilasters.

The 400 block of Vincent Avenue

THE BLOCK: The 400 block of Vincent Avenue, on the even-numbered or west side of the street, between Avenue E on the north and Northline on the south, in the Metairie Club Gardens neighborhood of Old Metairie in Jefferson Parish. Nearby is the 1920s-era Metairie Country Club.

A few blocks to the north is Metairie Road, which is lined with cafés, stores, grocers, schools, churches, and every imaginable amenity. An agency called the Old Metairie Commission reviews requests for demolitions and major additions and alterations in this Jefferson Parish community. Trees are valued and ordinances are in place to protect them.

THE HOUSES: Four fine 1920s-era houses, three of which share elements of the Mediterranean Revival style and the fourth embodying the Colonial Revival style. All are brick or stucco—as opposed to wood—and each is situated on a wide lot and set far back from the sidewalk.

ANATOMY OF THE BLOCK: As I explore Metairie Club Gardens, I find the perfect block for a walk when I discover the 400 block of Vincent Avenue, where every house on the block appears to date to the early days of the area's development.

I begin near the corner of Northline in front of a vividly painted Mediterranean Revival raised-basement house and walk north toward Metairie Road. The house has dramatic arched-top casement windows, a generous front porch, steps that lead up the side of the porch, and multiple sets of French doors.

The next house, a two-story stucco villa with a red tile roof and arched openings, also has Mediterranean Revival character.

Its facade centers on a handsome entry detailed with tall pilasters reaching up toward a second-floor balcony. Recesses on the left side of the house on the first and second floors create sheltered porches, which are accessed by French doors. The rounded arches on the first-floor porch mirror the form of the windows on the right side of the house. The porch on the upper level has a swing, and I imagine someone enjoying many an evening there, shaded from the afternoon sun.

I walk on to study the red brick house next door, a well-executed Colonial Revival. The unpainted red brick, the rectangular footprint, the side-gabled roof, and focus on the entry all exemplify the style, even if the facade is asymmetrical rather than the more traditional symmetrical. Detailing of the entry is especially complex—Corinthian columns support the roof over the door, pilasters flank the door in the plane of the facade, and dentils line the entry cornice.

A beauty with a green tile roof is located next door on the corner, set in a sea of emerald green grass. White, stucco, and two stories tall, it shares elements with other houses on the street, like the arched openings at ground level, the roof overhang, and casement windows (here in triplet). Wings on either side of the entry arcade have contrasting rooflines, hipped on the left, gabled on the right.

Farnham Place

THE BLOCK: The odd-numbered or east side of Farnham Place in Old Metairie in Jefferson Parish, between Metairie Road on the north (where its entrance is marked by a pair of stately columns) to the railroad tracks on the south. Given that no through streets interrupt Farnham Place, it's fair to say that the street itself is one very long block, facing the broad neutral ground planted with flowering shrubs and sprawling oaks.

THE HOUSES: Eighteen gracious homes, many of them brick and two stories tall, set well back from the street. Most were likely built in the first few decades of the twentieth century, but there are also some mid-twentieth-century houses and one or two new homes built since Hurricane Katrina.

ANATOMY OF THE BLOCK: The stately pillars at the Metairie Road entrance to Farnham set the tone for what's to come. I start at Metairie Road and walk south, passing a Dutch Colonial Revival house, then a white Colonial Revival house with a forecourt of crushed limestone. A red brick house with a dramatic two-story side gallery follows.

I stop when I get to the ivory-colored center-hall with lime green shutters and Ionic columns and a central roof dormer. I suspect this house was built after Hurricane Katrina, for it is the only house on the block in this style and is a contemporary interpretation of an historic house type. Next to it, I find a warm brick Colonial Revival house with a barrel vaulted cornice.

A few houses down, I stop again, this time in front of another two-story red brick house with a well-articulated front porch and central entry. The next house has a semicircular portico in front, supported by round tapered columns. The front door features a fan transom above it.

As I continue, I pass several houses, then pause in front of a personal favorite. It's a two-story stucco house with French doors, arched-top openings, and batten shutters, and feels a bit like a European farmhouse or country home. Along the front walk, paving stones are laid in a diamond pattern with groundcover in between, clever and playful. A vine, perhaps a variety of wisteria, is trained to climb on the front, complemented by a pair of expressive topiary urns.

By now, I'm still a few houses away from the railroad tracks and the Metairie Country Club golf course beyond, but I cut my walk short to savor again several houses I have already passed.

The 600 block of Codifer Boulevard

THE BLOCK: The 600 block of Codifer Boulevard, on the even-numbered or south side of the street, between Helios Avenue on the east and Hesper Avenue on the west, in the Bonnabel Place subdivision of Old Metairie in Jefferson Parish. The Bonnabel Civic Association traces the neighborhood's origins back to 1836 when French-born chemist Henri Bonnabel bought a track of land on Metairie Ridge from Hypolite de Courval. Though Bonnabel worked with J. A. D'Hemecourt to draw up plans to establish a town to be called Bath, Bonnabel died in 1854 before his plans could bear fruit. Six decades later, his son Alfred Bonnabel took up the development of the land and created the Bonnabel Place and Old Homestead subdivisions.
THE HOUSES: A collection of six pre-World War II houses, mostly bungalows, and all retaining their early-twentieth-century architectural character. Most of the houses express the Craftsman style, though one hints at the English Cottage style and another features Neoclassical Revival elements. All occupy wide lots with driveways for cars.

ANATOMY OF THE BLOCK: I start at the corner of Helios and walk west toward Hesper, stopping first at a stucco cottage set close to the ground, with an asymmetrical plan and entry portico on the right side. It features a chimney on the front and a clipped gable of the roofline over the entry and on both ends. In lieu of a paved walkway from the sidewalk, the entry is accessed by stepping stones nestled in the grass.

To its right is a yellow bungalow with its front porch enclosed, a common practice employed to capture extra living space. It's the only one on the block that has been altered in any noticeable way. I move on to the blue house next door, where I detect the Neoclassical Revival style in the round and tapered Tuscan columns grouped together at the edges of the gable-fronted porch. Two pairs of French doors with fanlight transoms open to the porch, and I see the pattern of the transom repeated over the windows on the right side of the facade.

I love the cheery simplicity of the white and green paint scheme on the next house. Like the others, its facade is asymmetrical with an entry on the left side and a wing that extends out to the other side. Though the house body has wood siding, the forward face of the porch covering is stucco with applied ornamentation accented in dark green. The opening to the porch is a low, broad arch, echoed by the arch of the transom over the front door. Terracotta tiles cover the side steps and landing, where a love seat affords a comfortable place to sit.

I spot a Saints banner hanging in the front garden of the caramel-colored house a few steps farther down the block. The roof over the entry porch on this house is front-gabled with angle brackets, exposed rafter tails and some interesting wood accents. I realize that the house seems taller and more massive than its neighbors because of its gable-fronted roofline.

The last house on the block is a variation of the house to its left. Here the entry porch is to the right rather than to the left, and the porch columns consist of a cluster of tapered wood columns atop brick pedestals, an emblematic feature of Craftsman design.

SECTION V
BACK OF TOWN

    In local parlance, the term "Back of Town" means different things to different people. For some, it refers to the Sixth and Seventh wards; to others, it refers only to Tremé. Still others use it to refer to Mid-City or Broadmoor or a portion of Central City. It isn't uncommon to hear folks talk about "Uptown, Downtown, and Back of Town" when they want to express the wide-ranging nature of one thing or another.

    Herein, it is used to group together several neighborhoods with varied histories and demographic characteristics, but which share a defining characteristic. They all occupy lower-lying land away from the Mississippi River and natural ridges, which could not be dependably developed until technological advances made it possible to drain the land they occupy.

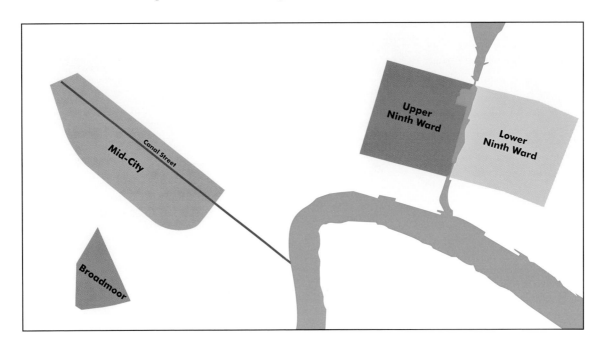

Mid-City

Mid-City was added to the National Register of Historic Places in 1993 and stretches along its Canal Street axis all the way from the Central Business District to the cemeteries between Conti Street and Interstate 10.

The district was originally a low-lying expanse of ground between the Carondelet Canal and New Basin Canal, which wasn't intensively developed until after a breakthrough in drainage technology and the subsequent construction of a pumping station at North Broad and Bienville streets in 1899. Mid-City derives its name from the fact that it was the approximate geographical center of New Orleans before the city's mid-twentieth-century expansion into New Orleans East.

One subarea of Mid-City, the Tulane-Gravier neighborhood, is located closer to the high ground of the natural levees of the Mississippi River than other parts of the district. It was therefore able to be settled earlier than the lower-lying portions toward the cemeteries, and it comprises some of the oldest buildings in the Mid-City Historic District. According to the National Register, the Tulane-Gravier area was well-developed prior to the publication of the 1883 Robinson Atlas, an early map of the city showing the location of buildings and predating the Sanborn Fire Insurance Maps.

The 2300 block of Palmyra Street

THE BLOCK: The 2300 block of Palmyra Street, on the odd-numbered or east side of the street, between South Miro Street on the north and South Tonti Street on the south, in the Tulane-Gravier neighborhood.

THE HOUSES: An eclectic mix of single shotguns, doubles, a camelback, and a Creole cottage.

ANATOMY OF THE BLOCK: I start at the South Miro Street end of the block and am deceived at first by what I think is a simple single shotgun with nicely detailed brackets, floor-to-ceiling windows, and cornices over the windows. I realize that the front porch has been removed (why would there be tall, walk-through windows if there is no porch to walk out onto?), so I figure the entrance has been moved to the side. I look and there it is, sure enough, as well as a camelback that isn't evident from the street.

Across the driveway on the South Miro side of the little camelback is the darling of the block, a Neoclassical Revival double. It is painted a sparkling white with cheery green cast-iron porch columns and railings, a color repeated on the gable window trim to accent that feature. The terracotta steps add the perfect color jolt to the composition.

A raised single shotgun is next door, also a brilliant white with handsome brackets. The arched-top windows and entry door transom tell me this is an Italianate house and confirms that it was likely built in the 1800s. Glossy green paint—slightly different in color from the bluer shade next door—accents the stoop railing and steps as well as the fencing.

There's a red brick stoop on the green shotgun next door, where a canvas folding chair occupies the landing. A metal awning provides shade for the stoop-sitter who, I imagine, uses this porch in the mornings or afternoons to visit with neighbors.

The hipped roof shotgun double next door is boarded. Someone has spray painted "Stop Do not Demolish" on the boards. I notice a door transom with elliptical glass—a shape I have come to associate with the Greek Revival era. I remind myself to confirm this idea with someone who knows more than I.

A Creole cottage on the corner has been pressed into service as a combination corner store and residence. It is boarded, too, but the store's sign remains and promises neighborhood staples like po' boys, cold drinks, snacks, and "hot plates."

The 200 block of South Galvez Street

THE BLOCK: The 200 block of South Galvez Street, on the odd-numbered or north side of the street, between Cleveland on the east and Palmyra on the west, in the Tulane-Gravier neighborhood. The block is just off of Canal Street and directly across from Deutsches Haus, a German cultural organization founded in 1928.

THE HOUSES: A mix of one- and two-story houses from a variety of eras, some converted to commercial use.

ANATOMY OF THE BLOCK: I start at the corner of Palmyra and stand on the shady neutral ground to take in the whole scene. The red and white building on the corner of Palmyra surely was a double camelback earlier in life; I recognize its form. But at some point the floor in the front portion was dropped to sidewalk level and the space converted to house Sam Jupiter Barber and Beauty Shop in the front and Durand's Tuxedo Consultants on the side. The building is painted a two-tone

scheme, a vivid red up to about four feet high, then gleaming white above. It's as cheery a place as you'll find on any New Orleans corner.

Next door, I study a pink and green single shotgun with milled brackets, drop-lap siding, quoins, operable louvered shutters, and floor-to-ceiling windows topped with cornices. I don't see steps to access the front porch on the front, so I suspect the entry has been relocated to the side.

In perfect chromatic harmony with the pink house is the green Neoclassical Revival sidehall house to its right. It has the same louvered green shutters covering its three front openings and even

fancier cornices above the windows and door. It also has stout box columns and a wide roof dormer with diamond-patterned glass, hallmarks of the early twentieth-century style. Because of the mix of features—some late nineteenth century and some early twentieth century—I puzzle over the home's past.

Next door, I see the green paint again, but this time applied as trim on a dazzling white sidehall single with brackets. Some purists don't consider sidehalls to be shotguns, insisting that the hallway automatically disqualifies it. However, I fall into the category of those who think of sidehalls as second-generation shotguns—a hall on one side of the house that affords access to the rooms, but rooms still arranged one after the other. This house has window screens featuring elaborate wrought iron grilles.

The two-story house next to the sidehall has been altered and acquired a cumbersome commercial facade; I really can't tell much

about its original appearance and move on. Next door is a raised house with attractive Craftsman details, especially the entry with its sidelights and transom.

A wide parking area separates the raised house from the third sidehall on the block, the house closest to Cleveland. A sign tells me that the New Orleans Safe Driving School does its business here. I spot a number of elements that this house shares with others on the block, but the arched tops of the windows and transom are enough to persuade me to call this one Italianate.

The 200 block of South Scott Street

THE BLOCK: The 200 block of South Scott Street, on the even-numbered or south side of the street, between Palmyra Street on the east and Cleveland Avenue on the west. The block is close to Canal Street and its streetcar as well as to a host of iconic New Orleans eateries like Mandina's and Brocato's.

THE HOUSES: The Craftsman style dominates on this block, which includes six double camelbacks, two two-story doubles, a gracious two-story single with a slight Queen Anne flair, and an Italianate sidehall shotgun (with a two-story rear addition).

ANATOMY OF THE BLOCK: If this block says "Mid-City" to me, what language does it use? I see a few things. First of all, the Crafts-man styling signals to me that most houses were built in the early twentieth century. Owners have used color to pick out architectural details and emphasize the charac-ter of the houses. The second factor is the predominance of shotgun

houses of all types, including dou-bles, camelbacks, sidehalls, and a two-story. Third, the presence of front yards set back is a spatial relationship that distinguishes the area from some of the oldest neigh-borhoods, where the house facades often meet the sidewalk.

I begin on the Cleveland Avenue end of the block where I find twin double camelbacks. Both have wide and detailed dormers on the one-story portion and a clipped (or flattened) gable on the camelback. Diamond-shaped panes of colored glass are present in the windows in the dormers and camelbacks, and pointy panes of colorful glass decorate the top sash of the windows on the front porch.

The third house is similar to the first two, but the dormer has a gable end and the porch columns and front doors are completely different. The fourth house is in the same family as the other three but with a few variations. Its front porch windows have a rounded top and spiderweb detail. Again, color draws my attention to the details.

The fifth house appears to be a single-family residence with a Queen Anne flavor to it, due in part to the curve of the wraparound porch. The branches of an oak reach out to it, but I can still make out the giddy colors of its gable.

The yellow house next door is a sidehall shotgun but with early-twentieth-century fluted columns. I can see it has an open gallery on one side, but I can't decide if the camelback at the rear is original or a later addition. No matter—it too has a side gallery on both levels.

A handsome two-story double is under renovation as I walk on. I realize that it has a clipped gable like the camelbacks closer to

Cleveland, and then it dawns on me that the attic vent is detailed exactly like the dormer and attic windows down the block. The renovator here has used a tomato red hue to emphasize the doors and sidelights.

There are three more houses to go before the end of the block. The first two exhibit characteristics of the other Craftsman-style houses nearby, one still retaining what is surely its original terracotta tile roof. That gets me thinking—did all of the houses on the block also have terracotta tile roofs once upon a time?

Broadmoor

The Broadmoor Historic District was added to the National Register in 2003 in recognition of its fine collection of early-twentieth-century architecture, especially its bounty of raised-basement houses. It is a pie-shaped area bounded roughly by Toledano Street and Washington Avenue on the east, Nashville Avenue on the west, and South Claiborne Avenue on the south. Surveys made immediately after Katrina suggest expanding the boundaries.

Some may have thought after Hurricane Katrina that Broadmoor would not be thriving as it is today. But when a green dot—signifying possible green space—appeared atop the neighborhood on an early post-storm planning map, neighborhood residents organized and launched a campaign not only to rescue their neighborhood, but to perfect it. Thanks to assistance from Harvard's Kennedy School of Government, the Broadmoor Improvement Association has helped hundreds of residents to return to the neighborhood and brought back a vast majority of its housing stock.

Throughout the neighborhood, lawns display signs announcing "Broadmoor Lives." No doubt about it!

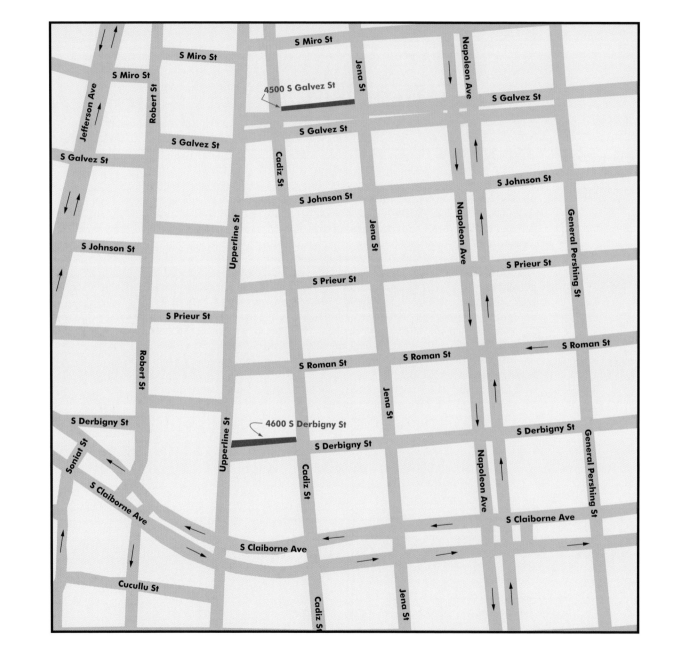

The 4500 block of South Galvez Street

THE BLOCK: The 4500 block of South Galvez Street, on the odd-numbered or north side of the street, between Jena on the east and Cadiz on the west. Houses on the block face a wide neutral ground where trees have been planted recently. Napoleon Avenue, the area's main thoroughfare, is just a block away.

THE HOUSES: A cluster of five houses, including two raised-basement types, a recently renovated ranch house, a Southern Colonial Revival home, and a charming cottage.

ANATOMY OF THE BLOCK: Starting at Cadiz, I walk east toward Jena and stop to study the first house. It's a Mediterranean Revival raised-basement house, a type of house unique to the Crescent City. Raised-basement houses are characterized by a full above-ground basement topped by the main living area and having a prominent set of stairs to the second floor. According to the National Register, one in four houses in Broadmoor fall into this category, so it isn't surprising to come across a pair of them on this block.

The first one I encounter has as many as three flights of steps. I notice how the runs of steps are broken up—a few steps, then a landing; turn right, then a few more steps; and so on. This device eliminates the need for a single imposing staircase and keeps the scale of the house at a human level.

The second house is a stylish updated ranch house. Many of my friends are aficionados of midcentury modern ranches and like them just as they are, but I am still developing a taste for the style. Here, however, the owners have gone out of the way to make their home esthetically appealing. They painted the entire exterior a glowing butterscotch color and added an entry overhang, sheathed in what looks like copper. The overhang gives the entry prominence and relieves the flatness of the facade. The awning shutters installed over a pair of horizontal windows also add dimension to the facade and impart a contemporary flavor to the exterior.

The third house on the block is another raised-basement house, this time interpreted in hearty red brick. Like the one on the corner, the steps are broken up into short flights to avoid the necessity of one massive staircase. The details on the door surround and the profile of the dormer make me think this is a Federal-style house, but I am not sure that the rounded-top windows would fit with that description.

The next house is a little unusual for the neighborhood. It's two stories tall but not a raised basement. The colossal columns that stretch all the way from the first-floor porch to the roof overhang convey a monumental feel to the building. I see that the second-floor porch has been closed in, but in my mind's eye, I envision the house without the enclosure.

The cottage adjacent is the polar opposite of the columned beauty. Modest in size, human in scale, the house has a portico over the front porch that welcomes visitors into the shade. Multiple rooflines and wings break up the massing of the home, making it feel approachable.

The 4600 block of South Derbigny Street

THE BLOCK: The 4600 block of South Derbigny Street, on the odd-numbered or north side of the street, between Cadiz Street on the east and Upperline Street on the west.

THE HOUSES: A row of six early-twentieth-century bungalows, two immaculately cared for, another pair of houses under renovation, and two more awaiting attention. Each house is modest in size, features a front porch—whether screened in, open, or enclosed—and displays one or more of the signature elements of the Craftsman style. All but one or two still bear a Katrina tattoo when I visit two years after the storm.

ANATOMY OF THE BLOCK: I start my walk near the corner of Upperline and head east toward Cadiz. On the very first house, I notice a deep roof overhang and multiple short columns set atop brick pedestals. A tree, a sweet olive I think, provides shade for the screened porch.

Next door, I recognize another hallmark of the Craftsman style in the bank of triple windows. The porch on this one is fully screened, and the steps are situated on one side of it rather than in the front. I don't see the tall skinny chimney until I walk around to the other side—the hurricane made a lot of trouble in Broadmoor but didn't knock over the chimney pot! No Katrina tattoo here; a coat of brilliant white paint has erased it.

The house on its right has a notably tall and narrow roof dormer, a bit atypical of the Craftsman style. The dormer flares out at the base, giving it a pyramidal shape. As unusual as it is, I bet it's original, based on the extreme overhang and rafter tails of its roof.

I walk toward the neighboring house and note details including a stucco gable with a horizontal gable window, arrowhead-gable edge boards, and elegant columns. Steps lead to the side of the front porch and the porch is open. However, the most unusual feature is the exuberant wrought iron railings on the porch, the pattern echoed in the window box support.

Workers are still busy at the fifth house when I visit. I spot a temporary pole in the front yard, and I see a new garden has been planted. Whereas the bricks were left unpainted on a few houses I passed, here they have been painted an energetic terracotta color. The full-width front porch has been enclosed with glass, maybe to create more square footage. I walk farther and see that this house has an unusual roofline, two intersecting gabled roofs at right angles to one another.

The house at the corner of

Cadiz repeats elements of other houses on the block, including an open porch, multiple columns in groupings, a stucco gable with horizontal gable window, and even the arrowhead-gable edge board. I study the casement windows on the porch and observe their distinctive diamond-shaped panes of glass. Flanking the front door are single, fixed panes of glass, but it's my hunch that there used to be sidelights there that matched the casement windows on the porch.

Ninth Ward

When the Industrial Canal was built in the early 1920s, it divided the Ninth Ward (one of New Orleans' seventeen voting districts) into two segments: the Upper Ninth Ward, upriver or west of the Canal, and the Lower Ninth Ward, downriver or east of it. Technically, the Ninth Ward voting district extends from Lake Pontchartrain on the north all the way to the Mississippi River on the south. But the terms "Upper Ninth Ward" and "Lower Ninth Ward" are used locally to refer to much smaller areas.

West or upriver of the Canal, the Upper Ninth Ward is considered to be the area bounded roughly by Florida Avenue on the north, St. Claude Avenue on the south, the Industrial Canal on the east, and Press Street on the west. The Bywater Historic District is immediately to the south.

East or downriver of the Canal, the Lower Ninth Ward is considered to be the area bounded roughly by Florida Avenue on the north, St. Claude Avenue on the south, Jackson Barracks on the east, and the Industrial Canal on the west. The Holy Cross Historic District is immediately to the south.

Both the Upper and Lower Ninth Wards remained underdeveloped until the early twentieth century, when city-sponsored drainage projects made them suitable for habitation. Rapid residential development followed and was virtually complete by the 1950s. Although a few late-nineteenth-century houses can be found in these neighborhoods, most houses date to the early to middle decades of the twentieth century and reflect the types and styles of that era.

Post-Katrina projects have brought international attention to the neighborhoods, both of which were heavily damaged by flooding resulting from floodwall collapses on the Industrial Canal. In 2006, Habitat for Humanity broke ground on the Musicians' Village, a residential community intended to provide affordable housing for the city's artists. Across the Canal, the Brad Pitt-supported Make It Right Foundation has built contemporary sustainable houses for Lower Ninth Ward residents displaced by the flooding.

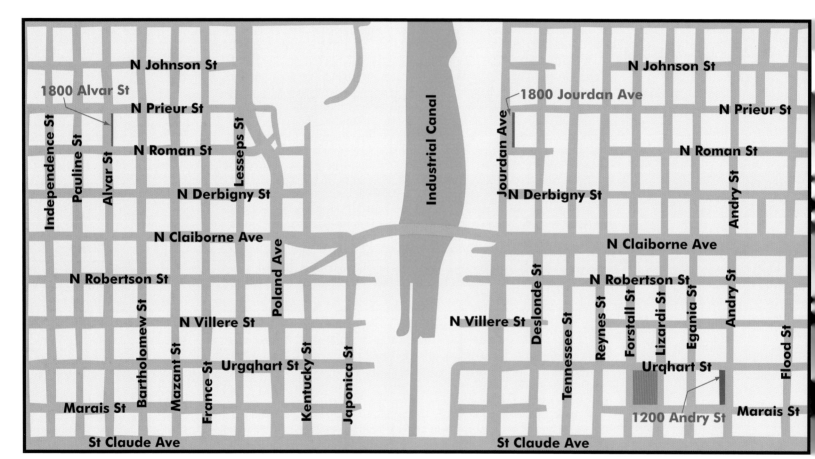

The 1800 block of Alvar Street

THE BLOCK: The 1800 block of Alvar Street, on the odd-numbered or east side of the street, between North Prieur Street on the north and North Roman Street on the south, in the Upper Ninth Ward. The block is one of many in Habitat for Humanity's Musicians' Village, built by volunteers from around the world on the site of a former school.

THE HOUSES: Eleven cheery-hued single-family residences raised high off the ground and personalized by their residents with fences, gardens, and painted accents that give each a personality of its own. Three different house types—some with gable fronts, others with porch overhangs—add rhythm to the block.

ANATOMY OF THE BLOCK: This isn't the first time I have visited a block on which the houses are related in style and form. I encountered a row of seven almost identical houses on Dumaine Street in Faubourg St. John, a row of shotgun houses that look like triplets on General Pershing, and so on. In fact, repeatedly I encounter either entire blocks of houses or small collections that I can tell are genetically related.

Even though every house in the 1800 block of Alvar Street is brand new, the block reminds me nonetheless of those other blocks and of how buildings change over time. I see the process has already begun here, for one resident has installed an iron fence on the front property line whereas another has installed a chain link. Several houses already have trees and gardens planted in their front yards. I see that some residents have painted the handrails on their front steps and that others have left the wood natural.

It is immediately evident from looking at the block that its history is just starting to be written. Who knows how different from one another these houses might look a hundred years from now? Odds are, by then, it will take an old house geek like me to puzzle over them and figure out what they had in common when they were first built.

As I study the block, I realize that I am looking at three distinct house types, repeated and slightly tweaked to make up a varied set. One of the three types has a broad front gable projecting out over the front porch to provide shade. A second model has the same broad gable, but terminating at the front wall so that a porch roof has been added to shade the front porch.

The third, more complex type features a double gable design, a smaller gable extending over the entry porch with a wider one behind it. Sometimes the porch appears on the left and at other times on the right, making the houses mirror images of one another.

Color may be the most powerful personalization tool employed on the block. I count at least eight body colors, ranging from pale yellow to dark purple with mocha in between. It occurs to me that even identical houses look different from one another when distinguished by color.

The 1200 block of Andry Street

THE BLOCK: The 1200 block of Andry Street on the even-numbered or west side of the street, between Urquhart Street on the north and Marais Street on the south, in the Lower Ninth Ward. The block is just a few hundred yards north of Holy Cross and St. Claude Avenue, where commercial activity has been partially restored. Many of the houses on the block appear to be occupied and another is actively under renovation.

THE HOUSES: Eight houses, primarily from the early to mid-twentieth century. Some sit right at the sidewalk and others are farther back on their lots. Seven of the eight houses exhibit one kind of Craftsman detailing or another, even one of the two brick houses. A raised-basement house is elevated to accommodate a street-level basement, but the eighth house, a brick ranch, is built at grade, a common practice at midcentury.

ANATOMY OF THE BLOCK: I start at the corner of Marais and walk north, drawn by the gold-colored house at the corner. It's freshly painted and perfectly manicured, an Arts and Crafts treasure with a stained-glass window in the gable, angle brackets, and tall brick columns supporting the porch roof. The owner has installed slate on the porch deck and steps as well as a new iron railing to spiff it up.

I see that the neighboring house is under renovation. It appears to be a Craftsman bungalow, judging from the roofline and details like flared columns atop brick bases and the exposed rafter tails. But it has been gutted to the degree that I can't be certain.

The single house next door features a cherub fountain in the front yard. Its neighbor is a hefty brick cottage with faint traces of Craftsman form, suggesting that a formerly wooden cottage was "armored" with bricks sometime in its past.

The only two-story house on the block is a Craftsman raised-basement a few steps farther on. It is boarded, and its Katrina tattoo is still surprisingly vivid, but it looks to be sturdy and sound, awaiting a renovator.

A neat and trim single follows. It displays Craftsman features like deep eaves and a front door with sidelights, but also an unusual set of steps—concentric circles of concrete, rather like a wedding cake. Next to the single is a freshly refurbished brick ranch, with its grass closely cropped and a recent coat of red paint on the roof overhang supports.

At the corner of Urquhart, the last house is a salmon-colored cottage with orange trim. Fluffy Indian hawthorn shrubs bloom on either side of the front steps and a "Welcome" sign hangs at the entry to the porch.

The 1800 block of Jourdan Avenue

THE BLOCK: The 1800 block of Jourdan Avenue, on the odd-numbered or east side of street, between North Prieur Street on the north and North Roman Street on the south, in the Lower Ninth Ward directly across from the Industrial Canal levee and floodwall. The day I visit in early 2008, the Make It Right project has just been announced and bright pink boxes are scattered around the site where homes will be built.

Unlike other blocks I have toured, this one is already in the process of vanishing, its scaffolding being called into service for Carnival viewing stands, and the pink sheathing for conversion into products that will help finance the rebuilding of the neighborhood.

THE HOUSES: There are no real houses on the block, but to me the abstract shapes of the boxes call to mind house types familiar in New Orleans neighborhoods. Intended or not, the installation appears to employ the basic volumes of shotgun houses and Creole cottages and to recombine them in unexpected ways. All occupy a field cleared for the project and are lit from within using solar energy.

ANATOMY OF THE BLOCK: Although I have been here before, earlier in the day, this is my first encounter with the drama of the boxes glowing at dusk. I am unprepared for how amazing they look, illuminated from within and without. Something about the vivid, Technicolor boxes and the brooding evening clouds moves me.

I begin at the corner of North Prieur Street and note that some of the lots at the corner are empty—no pink boxes, no steps to nowhere, no piers, nothing. It reminds me how complete the devastation was here. A few steps farther, though, the collection of glowing forms begins.

First, I see what reminds me of a classic Creole cottage, with a pitched roof that slopes toward the street. Next, there is a shotgun, narrow end to the street, roof sloping to the sides. I know the shapes aren't meant to be taken so literally, but I can't help seeing references to familiar house forms.

The third "house" is a departure from the traditional. Like many of the contemporary houses proposed for the site, the structure has a complex roof, sloping to one side in the front and toward the center in the back. Why not take the typical components and rearrange them in atypical ways?

The fourth calls to mind the city's many shotgun houses with side additions—two adjacent forms, one with a double-pitched roof. The fifth house looks familiar at first, but then I notice it has a single-pitched roof sloping steeply toward the back of the house. Taken together, the five compositions give the unmistakable appearance of a streetscape, however unconventional it may be.

Bibliography

Books

Campanella, Catherine. *Images of America: Lake Pontchartrain*. Mount Pleasant, SC: Arcadia Publishing, 2007.

———. *Images of America: Metairie*. Mount Pleasant, SC: Arcadia Publishing, 2008.

Campanella, Richard. *Time and Place in New Orleans: Past Geographies in the Present Day*. Gretna, LA: Pelican Publishing Company, 2002.

Chase, John Churchill. *Frenchmen, Desire, Good Children . . . and Other Streets of New Orleans!* Gretna, LA: Pelican Publishing Company, 2001.

Christovich, Mary Louise, Roulhac Toledano, Betsy Swanson, and Pat Holden. *New Orleans Architecture, Volume II: The American Sector*. Gretna, LA: Pelican Publishing Company, 1998.

Christovich, Mary Louise, Sally Kittredge Evans, and Roulhac Toledano. *New Orleans Architecture, Volume V: The Esplanade Ridge*. Gretna, LA: Pelican Publishing Company, 1995.

Friends of the Cabildo. *New Orleans Architecture, Volume VII: Jefferson City*. Gretna, LA: Pelican Publishing Company, 1989.

———. *New Orleans Architecture, Volume VIII: The University Section*. Gretna, LA: Pelican Publishing Company, 2000.

Toledano, Roulhac B. *A Pattern Book of New Orleans Architecture*. Gretna, LA: Pelican Publishing Company, 2010.

Toledano, Roulhac B., and Mary Louise Christovich. *New Orleans Architecture, Volume VI: Faubourg Tremé and the Bayou Road*. Gretna, LA: Pelican Publishing Company, 2003.

Toledano, Roulhac, Sally Evans, and Mary Louise Christovich. *New Orleans Architecture, Volume IV: The Creole Faubourgs*. Gretna, LA: Pelican Publishing Company, 1996.

Vogt, Lloyd. *New Orleans Houses: A House-Watcher's Guide*. Gretna, LA: Pelican Publishing Company, 2003.

Wilson, Samuel Jr., and Bernard Lemann. *New Orleans Architecture, Volume I: The Lower Garden District*. Gretna, LA: Pelican Publishing Company, 1998.

Web sites

Algiers Point Association: www.algierspoint.org

Bonnabel Civic Association: www.bonnabel.org

Broadmoor Improvement Association: www.broadmoorimprovement.org

Fontainebleau Improvement Association: http://members.cox.net/fontainebleau/

Greater New Orleans Community Data Center: www.gnocdc.org

Preservation Resource Center of New Orleans: www.prcno.org

Index